BRAND HEROES

find the one that works for your business

Dear Mark,

Meeting you ~ an absolute pleasure.
I hope you enjoy the book.

All the best,
Kd

Inverness, 4th April 2018 (Wednesday)

vol. 01

Klementyna de Sternberg Stojalowska

CONTENTS

CONCLUSION   195

INTROSPECTION   204

ACKNOWLEDGEMENTS   211

ABOUT THE AUTHOR   212

INTRODUCTION

WE HOLD THE KEYS TO OUR BRANDS' SUPERPOWERS

We go into business to do what we want to do. What we love, what we believe in. To create value and to find clients that resonate with our values.

It all starts from us – it all begins from you.

You and your personal brand as a founder are the seeds of your business brand. The two need to be aligned. Otherwise, the chances for success are undermined. When personal brand and business brand are synchronised, you get the Holy Grail, the Fountain of Life, the Force, the cold fusion – you harness the power of the universe.

Choose your favourite metaphor or, better still, add your own.

When this happens, your business elevates your personal brand and your personal brand fuels the business. You build and nurture networks, find clients, inspire teams and engage business partners. They are drawn to you. I have seen it. The signs are so very much visible, if you know what to look for.

I find business networking meetings a great testing ground and I use a simple enough test to see if a brand hero stands before me or if I am talking to someone whose powers are yet to be awakened.

My brand hero test question is simple: *"So, what do you do?"*

I will hazard a guess that you have asked that question yourself and have been asked yourself as well. The answer may be simple but the manner in which people answer it, tells all. There are so many ways to say *"I am an accountant / a lawyer / a dentist / a graphic designer"*. What I always hope to hear is *"I am THE accountant / lawyer / dentist / graphic designer for [specific issue] of [specific type of person]"*. And I hope to see them light up. To hear words coming easily and to see a smile reaching their eyes. I encourage you to try it next time during such a meeting. It is a very interesting experiment to observe how people react to such a basic question about their profession. If you meet a person whose personal and business brands are aligned, you will hear their heart sing.

You can tell that with their talent they can conquer the world. They are heroes within their niche. And you believe them.

Have you ever met someone just like it?

Make a note of who that is, it will be useful during further ponderings.

When you do, do you think to yourself *"I wish I was like that, it would be great if I had it in me"*?

Please do not panic if I tell you that you **do** have it in you.

You do

We so often think that the grass is greener on the other side. I know I sometimes do.

I noticed that in those moments it is so easy for me to lose perspective and focus on what I am not, what I do not know yet, what I haven't done. When I look at others I notice their accomplishments with no trouble. From a distance it is so easy to see a big picture. It is easy to admire how they fulfil their potential. My brand heroes are moving so fast. In comparison, I seem to be standing still.

It is a matter of perspective and a matter of focus

My heroes were, and are, from all industries and of all sizes. Whether they are starting as solopreneurs or are an established international brand, they seem good enough to fulfil that potential and are often in absolutely THE best place to make the next step to developing and growing their brand. I think to myself *"S***t, how did they get to that place?"* I realised that if I figure this out, I will be able to find a way to get there with my business. This is why I wrote this book, to figure out what makes a brand hero tick: their thinking and their actions and how to make it happen for me.

I believe it could be of use to you, too.

AS GOOD AS IT GETS

Whatever stage of entrepreneurial development you are at –
whether you are an entrepreneur, a business owner or are still self-
employed – it is OK. The stage you are at right now is the best place
to make the next step towards becoming a brand hero. Never fear :)

Turn your brand thinking on

There is no point in waiting until you are bigger, better, faster,
stronger, with a bigger team, with more funding, with new premises,
or until next Wednesday. You are not just going to one day wake up
as a brand hero, for the powers are already within you. You need a
catalyst, a nudge to turn your brand thinking on and harness your
powers.

Today.
Now.
Here.

This book is filled with descriptions of when and how various
business and personal brands turned their brand hero thinking
on; still, let me give you a quick example right now to illustrate the
process.

YOUR FAVOURITE THING IN THE WORLD

I used to belong to a networking group that met on a weekly basis
and each week we had a minute to introduce ourselves and one of
us would have 10 minutes to present details about their business.
One of the members, Nicholas Challen, was a procurement
specialist, and each time he would talk about utilities and energy.
Important subjects, but going through bills is hardly exciting. Once
he mentioned he used to work closely with restaurants and high-
end London hotels as a food supplier, and when he talked about that
subject, although only for a minute, the room fell silent. That was
his best 60-second presentation ever. I had known him for a year
by then and that was the first time I'd heard about this aspect of his
work. He just never talked about it. Yet his passion and knowledge of
the subject was evident. It was full of facts, stats, recommendations
and all. A joy to witness.

One other colleague from this group and I picked up on that and commented. Indeed, whenever I saw this gentleman I mentioned something about his procurement for food-related businesses. It did not happen instantly, indeed it took him another two years to really go for that niche and today he has written a book. At the time of writing, he is redoing his website and he is finally in his element. He still uses the skills that he used to apply to a wider market but now his efforts are just more focused. It is easier for him to position his business, talk about it and himself; not to mention that, being a foodie, he is even more credible. I had the pleasure of working with him on the strategy of a refreshed brand, but it is his passion and expertise that makes it work. He still works hard on developing his business and I help him develop his brand. Just now it feels right – with all brand elements in place, it is a bit easier. Nicholas was brave enough to follow his passion; we aligned his business with it and it clicked. It made him ready to elevate his business higher.

Can you think of such a person within your network? Perhaps you are one.

I believe I am.

Here's why.

You are a force and you can choose a side: the light or the dark

There are always two ways of looking at things: how to do them and how not to. For years I subscribed to the latter. This meant I was quick to classify my master's degree in Sociology as just a degree, years of advertising agency experience as a job, and the way I worked with my clients as "just my way of doing things" that I do not have to share with anyone, ever. My background is copywriting and 'creative copywriter' was my first serious job title (if you disregard a summer job in a clothes shop). I learned on the job; I started with straplines and headlines, then moved on to whole articles, then learned how to work with a creative brief to generate ideas for campaigns (radio, TV, big name magazines, you name it...) and was a member of a team that actually delivered them as well. The agency I worked for had a wide selection of clients and I learned how to develop campaigns with both local and national reach, for new brands and established ones. First of all, we always approached businesses as brands, and that thinking stuck with me, although I did not realise it at the time. To me it was just the way I did things. So, when I moved to the UK and started on my own – first as a freelance copywriter, then self-employed – I continued to think about each and every business I encountered as a brand. I then noticed that businesses do not necessarily think about themselves as such. Still, even for purely copywriting assignments, I applied my branding methodology. If you want to deliver effective copy, you need to know what your client is trying to say, right? So I would spend two or three days analysing their existing collateral materials (if they had any), studying their competitors, examining target audience, defining tone of voice, discussing my client's past and their business's future, and then I would proudly present a piece of copy, keeping all that research for myself. That was just how I did things.

So, yes, there are two ways of looking at things: how to do them and how not to. Both require effort, so focus on the one that may benefit you most. If you are not doing it yet, you can begin today.

This book is a sort of *thank you* to brand heroes who helped me realise that. Now it is my turn.

BRAND HERO PROFILE

A brand hero is a model of features and characteristics, which I formed during my experience and through working with clients in various markets, countries and specialisations. You may compare it with personality types, where readers identify their own temperaments as being of a certain disposition (introvert or extravert, blue or yellow, etc.). Similarly, some brand heroes' traits are more prominent. I identified 10 main distinct elements that make up my brand hero model. It is a theoretical concept but one I distilled from interactions with real people on my professional journey. (I define them below, and at the end of the book you will find all 10 traits analysed in context of specific case studies.)

For me, a brand hero is an entrepreneur – one who organises resources and benefits from their exploitation – who wants to change the world and leaves their mark on it with their beliefs and actions. They are creating their own brand space around them. An

Well, it took an external perspective to point out that 'my way' is actually my methodology; a process that I could open up to my clients to serve them better. This remark prompted an evolution of my thinking. It took a while to pluck up courage to start talking about 'my way', but I said it and made it happen. It also took a while for me to rework the way I approached my experience. I analysed my education, experience and heritage, and decided to look at my Polish background as international experience, my master's degree in Sociology as training in catching trends, and my English (a second language) as a skill making me even more sensitive to how people use the language and their cultural preferences. I learned how to appreciate my background and worked out how each element of my personality and experience complements my brand.

area where ideals lead to good practices and inspire people/others to do better; both internally, within the organisation, and externally, through inspiring, educating, entertaining, and stimulating consumer choices that enrich experiences and lives.

Brand hero thinking is not limited to price, product, service and fame. Brand heroes are thinking about ecosystems, strategies and a better future – they remember about the world without forgetting about themselves. When they are young (in a business experience sense of the word) they often feel overwhelmed by what is possible. Yet, they see the growing scope of possibilities and they act despite the fear. The feeling of stepping out of their comfort zone is often present – especially when they consider their mission and vision. The more they think about it, the more it seems like a set of logical steps rather than elements of unachievable greatness someone else, someone bigger, better, wealthier, is destined to.

Here I am presenting my brand hero thesis: archetypical elements that this construct holds:

1. Brand heroes inspire culture

We have only just met and I would like to put your mind at ease: you will find only a handful of references throughout this book, to ground it, but keep it liight enough to read with pleasure.

Deal and Kennedy[1] describe organisational culture as *"The way we do things here"*. Schein somewhat elaborates on it, comparing culture to a living organism born at the moment the enterprise begins; that organism grows on founders' *"ways of doing things"*. [2] This is how I understand culture as well; alignment of values and beliefs contributing to an environment promoting constructive behaviours, experiences, challenges and lessons.

I noticed that brand heroes, even if they are not using the word *culture*, create environments inspiring people to do their best. They attract talent, aspiration and emotion that propel their brand to greater heights. They inspire people – whether a client, a team member or strategic business partner – to be better, because they feel a part of the brand. They feel this brand is, to some extent, their own, a part of their persona.

1   Deal T. and Kennedy A. (1984) Corporate Cultures. in: Wilson F. (2004) Chapter 11: Culture. In: Organizational Behaviour and Work: A Critical Introduction. Oxford: Oxford University Press.

2   Schein E. H. (1983) 'The role of the founder in creation of organizational culture' in Organizational Dynamics, Summer 1983

2. Brand heroes stand proudly next to their logo

Brand heroes do not hide behind signs and straplines. Sharing their thoughts, both on professional and private matters (in an elegant way), seems to be a characteristic of a brand hero. They are not ashamed of their human element and that brings them closer to their audience. They teach by showing how things can be done and what can be achieved. They are past theory and well within the realm of practice. They will gladly tell you what they know and by looking at them and at their achievements, you can easily see they practise what they preach. In any case, practice comes first. And the logo is the emblem of that ethos, a symbol of those values and beliefs – an introduction to and indication of what hides beneath.

3. Brand heroes know how to learn from mistakes

Brand heroes do make mistakes and that does not stop them. It makes them evolve. They own their mistakes. They make the most of those mistakes and use them as lessons, as tools to improve their brands.

In many cases you can read about their less-than-perfect experiences in their blogs, vlogs and white papers. Error is a partner of endeavour and they are extremely active in trying new things out, so sharing both types of experiences – success and failure – becomes typical of their journey.

Nothing to be ashamed of; simply a part of another day in the life of a growing brand.

Brand heroes recognise that mistakes can help them make better decisions later. They can see that mistakes are inevitable and integral to being innovative and forward thinking. They also display the desire to spot them and fix them as soon as possible (hence they have a tendency to systemise, measure and evaluate). Mistakes are not seen as a bad thing, rather as an outcome – an outcome that highlights areas for improvement.

I so admire brands that welcome mistakes and even rejoice when they notice what can be advanced. No fear, no reservations – just motivation for action for there is something good to be done.

4. Brand heroes are open to knowledge

Brand heroes never stop learning: from experience, mistakes, each other. Personal development of the leader/creator is every bit as important as personal development of each member of the team. They are not afraid of hiring and working with people that are experts – they look forward to learning from people who know more. They appreciate knowledge as a tool to amplify their brands' influence and that approach permeates through all elements of the brand and embraces every member of the team.

5. Brand heroes are sanely passionate about what they do

Brand heroes' passion springs from their beliefs and is fuelled by unyielding determination to do what is right, not necessarily what is easy.

They are extremely knowledgeable about their industries; they are true experts, lucid about current trends and the context of their existence, as well as aware of what else there is to be done. They are often enviably in love with their place in the world; however, they have a deep understanding of the shortcomings of being an entrepreneur and that, if this is a bed of roses, the roses are thorny.

6. Brand heroes are purposeful

That sense of direction comes from clarity of vision and a deep understanding of mission. Irrespective of the size of their business and business maturity, brand heroes have grand goals. These plans are giving them direction and focus, the ability to judge whether they are on track without delay. They have their brand core defined and as such it gives their decision-making swiftness and makes their efforts even sharper. That's part of their creative advantage. Look for elements that resonate with your brand's personality, take notes and I hope this will help you develop your brand further.

7. Brand heroes have a firm grasp of reality

Deep understanding of where they stand in the scheme of things is another characteristic of brand heroes. Wherever they are, however small they are when they start, this is just a description of today. They need to have it to realise what steps need to be taken in order to take them to where they need to be tomorrow.

Understanding and appreciation of what they stand for, their values, what they wish to express, runs deep within their business structure and underlines their activities. Their identity may not yet be perfect, but they know what they want to express and they are working on making themselves known for all the right reasons. Their motivation is greater than money and that helps them survive the difficult start-up moments.

This also makes the relationships they develop with their clients stronger. And they invest in developing relationships with clients. They know what their clients are going through, often they have traversed similar tracks. They utilise that knowledge. They stay relevant by constantly reviewing their clients' problems and adapting their brand solutions to fit, anticipate and inspire.

8. Brand heroes have appetite for solutions they can deliver today

Creating value is the core of the activity of brand heroes; they work hard to be able to deliver their promises. They grow their presence in their categories by increasing the value of relationships with their clients, one client at a time. Good product, good service – yes, that is a given, and they think about the *"what else can we do?"* aspect. What is more, they deliver that *"what else"*. They do not stop at generating ideas. They do not shy away from bringing them to life. As such, they make a real difference to the market of *"that'll do"*. Little by little, and sometimes in big leaps, they make the world better.

9. Brand heroes champion cooperation

Brand heroes are confident of their own knowledge, and develop their intellectual property and culture. This enables them to look at other brands as potential business partners. Knowing what differentiates them in the marketplace allows them to search for and build more effective and lucrative associations, ones that allow for cross-pollination of industries, ideas and technologies. They bake a bigger pie, rather than worry about the crumbs from a smaller one, and look at complementary skills allowing them to deliver a more comprehensive solution to the client.

They usually think about cooperation, not competition. They are aware of the technology and market trends and focus on creating their own spaces, where they lead and inspire.

10. Brand heroes grow

To me branding is a process; never complete, constantly evolving – brand heroes are also never *done*. Even those, perhaps even especially those, with international presence see themselves as brands in the making. This is a reflection of their understating of the environment and embracing its evolution. There is a desire to be a part of the change, a strong opposition to being left behind.

I see brand hero characteristics in people in enterprises in all industries and at various stages. It may surprise you, but I believe even a pre-start-up can be a brand hero. That is because I believe we are all brands, personal brands, to begin with. We become a business brand from the very second we entertain a thought of launching a business venture.

You may have guessed that I consider you, dear reader, as a brand already, and perhaps should you wish to follow this path, a brand hero in the making. I invite you to analyse your own brand with these characteristics in mind, even before you continue to read all the profiles included in this selection. You may find brands, not necessarily within your own industry, which overcame challenges you may be facing at this moment. I hope this book will inspire you to develop your brand further.

THE METHOD

This book began as a social media experiment I devised to give myself confidence to start publishing online. I had an idea to interview people I admire, individuals who are great personal brands and business brands. Some of them are changing their world locally, some nationally, a few even internationally. Whatever their reach, I was interested in what they are doing right.

Always look at the bright side of the brand

I believe that it's easy to find articles and blogs that show all the difficulties of doing business. Therefore, I wanted to show the good, the exciting and the *"it-is-worth-overcoming"* part of entrepreneurship. I wanted to create a portrait of businesses others can feel optimistic about and shine the light at the 'behind the scenes' element as well.

I knew I wanted my meetings to have an atmosphere of informal conversation, but I also wanted to make sure all aspects of brand development would be covered (brand creation, naming process, mission, vision, values, market context...). The easiest way was to design a checklist. I started with main areas and then added more details.

WARM-UP QUESTIONS (purpose: to create a space for a comfortable conversation)
Getting into a zone of thinking about your own brand takes a moment and I found having a light opening section is a good way of easing into it. It helps to break the ice and set the tone of conversation. It helped me, as an interviewer, to slow down from the buzz of a busy day and to get into the mood of the conversation, and it also helped my heroes to feel a bit more comfortable with me, especially when this conversation was the first of its kind, and not all of them were used to talking about themselves and their brand in this way. The more comfortable atmosphere I was able to create, the more in-depth insights we were able to discover.

NAMING (a rose by any other name would smell as sweet... or would it?)
I was looking for rationale behind the name of the brand: was it named after the founder, the market category of the product, the product itself, the location of the business, or was it a random word or phrase? I wanted to find out what were their initial thoughts behind the name, what was it that they wanted the name to represent... in addition, I was interested in discovering if they spent much time on choosing the name – or was it just a spark of inspiration? Also, who was responsible for suggesting the name: themselves, a committee, someone else entirely, or had it perhaps been inspired by a story or a situation?

VISUAL IDENTITY (utilitarian fashion statement)
I wanted to analyse the connection between the verbal and visual identity of my heroes and how both elements influence each other:

which came first, who was involved in the process, how long did it last, do they consider it finished, were there many iterations; perhaps it grew organically and still evolves, what did they want the colours and shapes to convey, are they working with a dedicated team or overseeing the design and implementation themselves?

MISSION & VISION (the past, present and future of the brand)
This section was created to help focus the interview on the space the brand occupies in the market and to understand why they do what they do. I wanted to understand the context of the organisation and the motivations of people involved. To better grasp the ideas of the brand and its plans for the future, I investigated its past, its origins – in the hope that it would give me context of what makes them want to change the world and what (and who) inspires them to pursue their goals.

VALUES (what really matters to the brand and what makes it valuable to the client)
Often, especially in the world of start-ups and young enterprises, values of the business brand reflect personal values of the founder. I wanted to check if this is still the case with my brand heroes. And, if so, are there any similarities between them?

I wanted to see if and how their values evolve, how clearly they communicate their values and how much that communication matters to them; what role values play in commercial success and in relationship building (both internally between employees and externally between business partners and clients).

There is a lot this section reveals. It turned out to be a great way to get a peek at the inner workings of my brand heroes.

QUICK-FIRE (speak your mind)
I found that by the time we (my brand hero and I) reached this section, at least 40 minutes had passed. To keep the momentum of the conversation, I selected a group of questions to use as a very loose implicit-association test: no overthinking, just speaking your mind. It was a fun way of diving into their personality and it gave me a good taste of the inner workings of their brands. Here I asked, quite boldly, about the good and the yet-to-be-improved aspects. My brand heroes were very brave and frank. There are no wrong

answers here, although there may be a few surprising ones.

Having a questionnaire meant I had a checklist that helped me introduce the project to my heroes. I often sent them the list of questions before our meetings, so that they had a certain idea of what to expect. I conducted my interviews as casual conversations, but they were focused and of reasonable length. Thanks to the plan I knew we needed to allocate 45–60 minutes for each interview or online conference.

PEN AT THE READY

Then it was time to write. To keep myself in check and make sure I didn't deviate from the subject too much, I developed a blueprint for the articles as well (headlines with detailed questions for each section). Having that blueprint also made my writing easier (I always outline a structure for every piece of copy I produce; it speeds things up and sharpens my mind). Although I had a list of questions and recorded most of the interviews/conferences, I did not want to simply transcribe them. I do realise it made things a bit more complex as it was still important to me for the interviews to be a starting point of a more involved brand evaluation. The goal for me was to make each interview into an individual story in a certain format that makes it easier for you, my dear reader, to compare, contrast and spot trends. You will find common themes running through this book, but each piece is a distinctive, separate tale of a brand hero.

Heroic countdown begins

Initially, I called the project *90 brand heroes challenge* as I was thinking of interviewing 90 brands in 60 days and writing them up on my website – the beginning was crazy, 15 interviews in the first week! I have to say, I only managed it because of the enthusiasm of my heroes. Their response has been fantastic. Some Brand Heroes I knew personally through networking and business development courses. I pitched the idea to them via social media and email. Others I approached out of the blue – writing to them via their websites. Some I discovered along the way, for example Fistful of Spice, who I met at a food festival and simply talked to about the project. And some of the brand heroes were introduced to me by another brand hero. This whole project allowed me to meet fantastic people – I am very grateful to them that they shared their insights and time with me.

It soon transpired that there was something bigger than just an online project brewing. Again, external perspective comes into play as I thought that this may be turned into a book, but people I interviewed began to ask if I was going to publish it in any other way than online and that seeded the idea in my mind and gave me courage to do so... and here we are.

What began as a blog turned into a tome that combines refreshed articles and their analysis. Stories included in this book were chosen to inspire and transpire my brand hero theory. You will find even more individual stories on my website, so watch this space.

HOW TO READ THIS BOOK

However you like, of course. I can tell you what was my structure in writing it, and you may choose to follow it.

Dear Reader, I encourage you to use the book as a workbook and put your own thoughts and ideas on these pages. That's what the slightly bigger margins are for.

This book is an overview of how brands come to life. It is, however, first and foremost an insight into the personalities behind these brands: their thinking, ideas, strategies, improvements, practices and plans. Please note, dear reader, this is not an academic publication – this content is analysed through my own experiences and tinted with my own personality – my own research bias. I am bringing here real-life stories of entrepreneurs who have done it and are continuing to deliver – and most of all this is my personal reflection of what I have observed and my impression of them on their journeys – and one I had immense pleasure putting together.

This book is, therefore, a compilation of brand portraits, or perhaps going as far as brand introspections. I was 'let in' and so I am now sharing with you an insider's view and my take on each of them.

While reading I encourage you to look for common themes in this book.

Turn the brand hero thinking on.

I invite you to look for elements that resonate with you and to seek different characteristics, beyond the ones I identified, that you find important and interesting. I also welcome you to share your thoughts and lessons from this book with me (you will find my ciontact details at the end of the book).

Business categories included in this publication are diverse, to say the least. The spectrum of entrepreneurial interest was simply too wide to categorise. Branding challenges, I find, are more connected to the business development stage rather than industry, which is why this collection is not divided into any particular sections and all brand heroes featured are categorised alphabetically. Each story is a full episode with its own independent plot. You can, therefore, read this book by opening it randomly, focus on a brand story of your choice, or devour it from cover to cover. If the reading inspires any questions, visit www.incelement.co.uk/brand-heroes-the-book and share your thoughts and questions. If it is in my power, I shall give you the best possible answer.

Even big brands were start-ups once.
If they succeeded, why not us?

You will notice that, with a few exceptions, the brands covered are boutique brands and not the Apples of this world. Why? These are brands I not only aspire to but can relate to as well. I am such a brand myself, both as Klementyna and as Inc Element, and for that reason I understand their challenges much better – simply because these are also my challenges. Their issues and ideas resonate with me. Their ways of overcoming problems are such that I can apply them in my own situations. Brands of the scale of Apple are today, in my mind, too abstract to the world of small and medium enterprises. I think that we will have a better chance of reaching their level when we focus on what's at hand. After all, they had to begin somewhere as well. It is an opportunity to get an insider's view, look at brand stories as clues on how to devise and implement better strategies here and now, when we are still seeds and not yet apples.

I hope you will find it entertaining and instructive. Enjoy.

LEIGH ASHTON, SASUDI

Name of business: SaSuDi (derives from SAles, SUpport and DIrection)
Founders: Leigh Ashton and Jonathan Mills
Years in business: Sasudi launched March 2016; however, its creators have been involved in sales and marketing since the mid eighties
Speciality: Educating and supporting small business owners in sales mindset
Location: London
Reach: National
Key to success: Good mindset supported by good strategy
Biggest challenge for businesses: Prioritisation and task completion; and cashflow
Greatest asset: Partnerships

THE ONE GOOD WAY TO SELL

If you are a business owner, chances are you have attended at least one sales-related seminar. I have. This was not a subject I was taught at school and, as a founder of a young business, I recognised this as a largely uncharted area.

Yet I found myself disappointed with most of them; I can say that today with the benefit of hindsight. I remember being left wanting. I was usually told to follow a script, make a cold call or send a defined number of emails per day. All participants were told the same thing, irrespective of the type of enterprise they – we – represented. And, my favourite, we were told 'to act confident' – with no hints as to how to actually become confident in selling.

The difference is significant.

Sasudi understands that and this is what put them on my heroic radar.

Sales – a big deal?

It is not only about the tools. It is not just about the strategies. It is not merely about accountability. It is not about the mindset alone, either. It is about all of those elements.

What it is about – through and through – is you. The person who wants to become a sales leader, to help a team or themselves.
"If you can change your thinking, you can change your behaviour. But you cannot change someone's behaviour without changing their thinking first. Thought creates the feeling that creates the action that gets you the result," says Leigh Ashton.

My way, your way, right way?

This change of focus has a profound effect. Where previous courses made me think *"I know nothing, I need to start all over,"* Sasudi told me *"Let's look at who you are and build from that."*

Many solopreneurs, and even seemingly confident sales people within larger businesses, associate the process of selling with fear, obstacles, pushing, force and uncomfortable situations. These are perceptions. Sasudi tackles all the myths associated with sales early on. They do it through their platform, built around five areas of interest: learning, inspiration, sales, community and customers.

Sales 360°

You have access to techniques that will improve your performance, tools to help improve processes – or, if you are at the beginning of the road, to start building them. It is a motivating safety net. It is an online tool that lives with you in real life, so to speak. All the tips and strategies are easily translated into behaviours, systems and actions. This platform is dedicated to small businesses and gives them clarity and guidance so needed at those early stages. It is very useful when it comes to keeping the overwhelming at bay. It allows the user to learn at their own pace and nudges them, at the right moments, to keep them going so that they do not stall.

It gives you a community, even though you are working individually. It offers support of real people, even though it is online.

It gives you a sense of accomplishment, even though you are still learning.

It helps you to be of value and generate value.

Person, team, brand

The first time I spoke with Leigh Ashton, co-founder of Sasudi, was over Skype. The second, in person. I have also attended her workshop. Her language is clear and her messages precise. When she presents facts and figures, she makes them inspirational – and when she chooses to read out a quote or present a philosophy, she makes it quite down-to-earth. Each time she came across as friendly, approachable, reasonable and kind. And so is the manner of her book and the structure of Sasudi's website. Clarity, reason and encouragement – all with a smile. This is why Sasudi appeals to me so much.

WHY A BRAND HERO?
It is not a one-fits-all solution. Yet Sasudi is flexible enough to help each user find the best way to improve their sales. It helps you work out the one sales strategy that works for you – your own.

Sasudi became a safe harbour for businesses wanting to improve their turnover but secretly being afraid of it. It is a healing space that helps you funk up your sales, let go of the fear, act with confidence and focus on creating an amazing business presence.

They are straightforward, they understand their audience, and they use the language that is easy to understand.

That is why Sasudi is my brand hero.

MY LESSONS FROM THIS CONVERSATION
1. Where you are now is the best place to move forward.
2. There's always a way out, just ask.
3. Techniques alone are not enough, you have to use them with the right intention, otherwise your actions will lack conviction and the outcome will not be satisfying.
4. One solution will not fit all, but you can most definitely develop the one solution that will work for you.

ELEMENTS OF A STRONG BRAND
- CLARITY
- ACCESSIBILITY
- EXPERTISE

INSPIRATION
- *Your Brain at Work* by David Rock
- *Find Your Lightbulb* by Mike Harris

MOTTO
"Taking the fear and dread out of sales for small business owners."

FIND OUT MORE
- Read *iSell* by Leigh Ashton
- Visit Sasudi's website and pre-register at sasudi.com
- Follow them on Google+ +SasudiSales/posts

What is the biggest value of your brand?

HEATHER BARRIE, HARRIE'S COFFEE

Name of business: Harrie's Coffee
Founder: Heather Barrie
Years in business: Since 2010
Speciality: ~~Decontaminaton (processes and product development)~~
Location: West Sussex (headquarters in Worthing)
Reach: National (via online platform and a great logistics company)
Services: Works with businesses to enable them to serve great coffee – a coffee that reflects their brand values and commitment to quality to their team and their clients. Harrie's also works with independent coffee shops and hospitality outlets to create a great, repeatable coffee experience by providing coffee beans, machines, training and coffee business consultations.
Biggest success: Partnership with a local artisan baker to release Harrie's Mocha Choca marshmallows and setting up a café within two weeks (from the initial phone call, to training the staff, to installation and opening day).

[handwritten annotation: this verse belongs in another story :) Harrie's speciality is coffee. awesome :) fdf.]

A SLOWLY BREWING REVOLUTION

I met Heather on the first day of a business accelerator programme.

I came early, saw a room full of round tables with six seats each, and was trying to figure out where I wanted to park myself for the day.

When I first saw her... let me start over: what I first saw, was a hat.

Then I looked closer at a person underneath and thought *"yes, I definitely want to meet her"*. So, I sat at the same table. My decision was definitely as good as her coffee.

Harrie's Coffee is an example of how a business can find its focus by making the most of an opportunity. This is how it began.

Not too long ago in picturesque Arundel, a mobile coffee bar was making commuters' very early mornings a little brighter by serving good coffee. Quality product and personal service was at the centre of operations even then. They sourced their coffee carefully – taste, origin, production process – all had to be ethically managed by the suppliers. When the supplier decided to sell, Heather was the first person he came to. Harrie's Coffee was ready to make that next step and introduce new services to their offering and become more than an award-winning mobile coffee bar... and so they did.

Three hats from the same designer

The business has three strands now:
- Quality coffee machines for business offices and hospitality outlets
- Wholesale and online coffee distribution
- Training and consultancy

Harrie's Coffee is an award-winning business recognised for their customer service and Heather herself won Business Personality of the Year in 2016 and got a special commendation for standing up for small businesses in the face of the Southern Rail strike. More accolades will come, no doubt!

Harrie's Coffee provides coffee, machines and training to independent hospitality outlets – and also delivers great coffee and equipment to offices and homes alike. However, Heather's personality shines through every one of them. Even the name encapsulates its creator's spirit; it's easy to remember and unique, so there was no conflict with existing brands when developing the business and moving online. Heather's hat is the brand symbol – a personal item became an icon for the business.

"They remember me," says Heather. I know I do.

Great expectations

Strong, honest, straightforward. That's Heather and that's Harrie's Coffee. She serves great coffee and works with her clients to enable them to do the same. Why?

Because Heather knows both ends of the business, and knows them well. The understanding of the customer service side of the beverage and what it takes to stand in the snow at the break of dawn to serve coffee – she has also run her own mobile café since 2007. She also knows the disappointment when you need a pick-me-up cuppa between meetings and you get a brown liquid of an unspeakable quality instead. She says no to that and no to poor customer service.

"I want consumers, wherever they go, to expect great coffee," says Heather. *"I want them to know that they don't have to settle anymore. No more shit coffee."*

It does not end with coffee – it starts there. When you work with her, when it comes to purchasing products or training, you get the best thing on offer. No compromises. She keeps in touch with her customers, creating a group of businesses offering great coffee.

Make your brand the strongest it can be

Heather's business idea could be franchised. There's just one little thing – it's such a strong brand because it has Heather in it. And if you want to start a coffee business or make good coffee part of your business, it will need her in it. Heather can show you how to make it work for you. She wants her brand and your brand to grow together, so you can count on her support and carefully designed processes that will help you grow – obviously, as long as you're prepared to give it your full attention as well.

"I will give you the product, the systems, the training. I will show you how to do it and how to do it well." ~ Heather Barrie

That's what working with Harrie's Coffee is designed to do – to enable all businesses to share a great coffee experience.

It is a slowly brewing revolution.

Let's crank up the heat.

WHY A BRAND HERO?

Bringing back boutique coffee outlets to the high street and encouraging business to serve the best is a quest I applaud. Getting rid of shit coffee is a quest I applaud. Creating strong coffee brands is a quest I applaud.

How great it is to see a business so comfortable with themselves that they are ready to champion variety and help others grow stronger as well. That's the definition of a strong brand.
Heather, I take my hat off to you.

MY LESSONS FROM THIS CONVERSATION
1. Helping others achieve can not only bring pleasure but strengthen your own position in the market
2. Have a personality and character and don't be afraid to show them
3. Say no to bad products and service, say no to shit coffee

ELEMENTS OF A STRONG BRAND
- PASSION
- QUALITY
- GOING THE EXTRA MILE (CUSTOMER SERVICE ETHICS)

INSPIRATION
- Anita Roddick
- Richard Branson
- Gandys Flip Flops
- Lego

MOTTO
"Be passionate (it will allow you to find people who love what you do and allow your idea to take off)."

DISCOVER MORE
- Visit harries-coffee.com
- Find them on Facebook @harriescoffee
- Locate Heather on LinkedIn (heatherbarrie1 "The Coffee Lady!")
- Instagram & Twitter: @harriescoffee

In what ways is your brand going that extra mile?

....
....
....
....
....
....
....
....

STEVEN BRIGINSHAW

Name: Steven Briginshaw
Years in business: Since 2012
Speciality: Business mentoring and education
Location: Berkshire
Reach: Global (clients in North America, Europe and Australasia)
Key to success: Be your authentic self and have clarity
Biggest challenge for businesses: Fulfilling their potential
Greatest asset: Teams, systems that support them, your community and list of clients/prospects

BACK TO THE FUTURE

Do you remember DuckTales? In the intro, Scrooge McDuck performs his daily money swim. This scene had a profound effect on a five-year-old Steven Briginshaw. So much so, that by the age of 10 he was adamant about becoming a bank manager.

"But I wasn't a bank manager, I just thought I wanted to be one so I could swim in the vault like Scrooge McDuck. :) At around 10 years old I realised bank managers don't do that. I then changed tactics," says Steve Briginshaw. It was not an obsession with money, though, but a fascination with the process of generating money that led young Steven to investigate what type of professions result in such riches.

He researched accountancy and the more he knew about it, the more he wanted to do it. That led to founding SJB Accounting, a company that rose above industry stereotypes and created its own brand. He was not done yet; what seemed like a pinnacle achievement turned out to be a stepping stone.

Author, accountant, mentor – whatever role Steven fulfils it is clear to me that his fascination with what good people can achieve with money is what keeps him helping them to rise to the top of their profession.

A new hope

I met Steven in 2013 when we both attended a business development course. When I put together this project, I knew early on he was one of the brands I wanted to talk to. I am pleased to say he was happy to help, and so we Skyped and talked about his past,

Branding and accounting have a lot in common. I only realised it after talking with Steven. Financial aspects – bookkeeping and accounting – are not just tedious clerical actions designed to make the life of the business owner harder, to the taxman's perverse satisfaction. These tools help brands act to their full potential. It is a challenge to find accountants that are brands themselves.

present and future.

Quiet confidence that moves mountains

Steve is brilliant at what he does. But, it was not always the same thing.

He has a fascination with bookkeeping, which he says *"is the cornerstone of the business"*. I have never heard anyone speaking about this subject in such an engaging manner. It is not about spreadsheets and receipts; suddenly we are talking strategy and meaning, and possible outcomes, and how to transform data into insight. I am listening with bated breath!

Steve knows how to extract data and teaches that to his clients. Steve is also a master of understanding the context of information. He appreciates the power of interpretation and he uses it to engage his clients, in the process empowering them to recognise and utilise their abilities. He makes a conversation about receipts thrilling – imagine what his influence is like when he talks about business transformation.

Be a force for good

Steve knows what it takes to develop a business and a personal brand. He builds both around value. Value that unites clients, supporting teams, business partners. He keeps developing and growing his brand for it is by making his most important brand better – himself – that he is able to help his clients even more.

He devised unique methodology Profits Principles™, wrote a book, and designed a portfolio of courses – and more is to come. He intends to grow an entrepreneurial academy that will benefit the next generation. With his efforts he is reaching not only beyond physical borders but also beyond those of time: he creates a legacy.

When we met, Steve introduced himself as an accountant, but he has always been a mentor. Never apologetic about his profession, with pride and fascination with the industry apparent in every sentence, with an unbelievably positive, engaging and sincere manner of speaking to – and with – clients. Like a proud dad. Shining light on others and staying incredibly humble himself.

Make it easier to be you

Not everyone is going to build a million pound business, and not everyone has to. But, everyone has the potential of achieving what they want to. As a mentor, Steve helps clarify goals and highlight processes, tools, and behaviours needed to achieve them. In one way or another, throughout his entrepreneurial journey, Steve has always oscillated around nurturing businesses' independence, giving them the tools to grow and highlighting their power to do good. That makes his brand consistent.

"Wasted potential, that's probably the worst thing in life. Seeing someone not achieving their best because of something external is such a travesty. I think it's really important to nurture entrepreneurs to make sure they get the light they need to shine."
~ Steve Briginshaw

Steven Briginshaw: business coach, mentor and author. From personal experience, I can also add that he is one of the most kind, tactful and elegant people I have ever met.

WHY A BRAND HERO?
Steve remains true to his own values. Because of that – through that – he helps his clients stay true to their brand.

He understands that fulfilling values or doing good through business growth is a process that can have many facets. He himself (at the moment of writing) is creating an entrepreneurial MBA course. The aim of this endeavour is to help current and future small business owners, over 24 years old, to build lifestyle impact businesses, enjoying what they do and paying it forward to help projects and causes they believe in. He is also working on a Youth Entrepreneur Academy to teach entrepreneurship to 16- to 24-year-olds, making entrepreneurship a realistic choice for them when they leave school.

He does good, and makes it easier to do good and feel good about it.

He is not done. Why would you stop something that brings you so much joy? For that, he is my brand hero. I am a fan and a student.

Steve published 'The Profits Principles TM' under a scheme 'buy one give one', which means with every book sold one schoolbook is donated to underprivileged children. He really means business when he talks about doing good.

Steve's WHY: "I get up every morning to help existing and future entrepreneurs create and run inspired companies – companies that are full of happiness, gratitude and purpose – so that together we have a deep and positive impact on our communities and our world."

MY LESSONS FROM THIS CONVERSATION

1. Find what you value above all else, find what makes you of value to others; if you see it as the core of your business, you have found the core of your brand
2. If you are true to your values, your brand will stay consistent as it grows and evolves
3. Your brand will evolve and that is a good thing; growing brand will allow you to do more good

ELEMENTS OF A STRONG BRAND
- KNOWING THEIR VALUES, THEIR TRUE SELF
- CLARITY
- DOING GOOD

INSPIRATION
- Warren Buffett
- Ricard Koch
- The E-Myth Revisited: Why Most Small Businesses Don't Work and What to Do About It by Michael E. Gerber
- Rich Dad Poor Dad by Robert Kiyosaki
- Start With Why by Simon Sinek
- The Millionaire Master Plan: Your Personalized Path to Financial Success by Roger James Hamilton
- The Secret by Rhonda Byrne

FIND OUT MORE ABOUT STEVEN
- Visit his website stevenbriginshaw.com
- Follow him on Twitter @SteveBriginshaw
- Read his book *The Profits Principles: The practical guide to building an extraordinary business around doing what you love*

In what way is your brand a force for good?

ANNIE BROOKS AND HELA WOZNIAK-KAY, SISTER SNOG

Two founders, two conversations, one brand: a double feature.

Annie Brooks
Name of business: Sister Snog
Founders: Annie Brooks (heart of the brand) & Hela Wozniak-Kay
Brand in business: Since 2002
Speciality: Keeping the beat behind the brand with an eagle eye on process and attention to detail on all aspects of service
Location: London (today)
Reach: International, if you're a social butterfly
Key to success: Being selective
Biggest challenge for businesses: Cash flow
Greatest asset: My business partner

Hela Wozniak-Kay
Name of business: Sister Snog
Founders: Hela Wozniak-Kay (soul of the brand) & Annie Brooks
Brand in business: Since 2002
Speciality: The creative spirit behind a sparkling platform for like-minded businesswomen so their brands can blossom and their businesses bloom
Location: London (today)
Key to success: Harnessing the power of being connected
Biggest challenge: Time management
Greatest asset: Sisters

IN A LEAGUE OF THEIR OWN

I came across Sister Snog before I realised I knew any of the members. First encounter – online. First impression – what a space! The language and tone of voice is what kept me on the page and had me diving in for more. Juicy words and phrases that winked at me. Shapes and shades ensnared the senses. Weaving through the pages made me lost for this world, this new reality. They are very carefully chosen, yet it feels effortless to be around them. The Sister Snog brand is like Harley-Davidson – if you have to ask, you will never know. You're either instantly in love with the brand – or not. And if you get it, you get it completely and want to join the tribe. There are no half measures. You want the proof – look at the footnote of the website: *"created with passion... designed with TLC..."* It makes you want to be a better business to be able to join them.

Sister Snog is a creation of the dynamic double act. Annie Brooks is the heart of the business, Hela Wozniak-Kay the soul. I talked to them individually. No conferring! Hela and I were 'ladies who lunch'. And a manic morning turned into a fantastic early afternoon. Annie and I conversed via Skype. No e-separation. Rather an instant connection. With both Hela and Annie there was sunshine. There was rhythm. Who could ask for anything more? This is the summary of my extraordinary experience of this out-of-the-ordinary brand.

The lunch that launched it all

Annie and Hela ran a branding consultancy. They'd made a decision to replace pitching with networking as a strategy to build their client portfolio at Snog The Agency. As well as throwing themselves into the London networking scene, on the first Friday of February 2002 they decided to invite two clients and two prospective clients to lunch.

The buzz around the table was both electric and contagious. So much so that First Friday flourished and became a hot date in the diary for a cornucopia of sassy businesswomen that culminated with the first ever Festive Friday lunch in December.

They say necessity is the mother of invention and the need for a refreshing alternative to the most traditional networking platforms became evident after a very short period of time. Sister Snog was a pioneer of the many vibrant business networks for businesswomen which are celebrated today. Its growth has been organic and evolutionary.

This is a brand that doesn't rest on its laurels and always has its next idea waiting in the wings. That's why Sister Snog is in a league of its own.

The network eve-olution

Back in the day, Annie and Hela networked like crazy. Although they loved connecting, they were not quite as enamoured with some of the networking conventions that did not agree with their spirit. The handing out of business cards, misspelt name badges (for Hela on a regular basis). Conventions for the sake of convention that often overlooked the true essence of relationship building.

What was needed was a new environment in which the evolution and feminisation of networking could happen. That was Sister Snog, which Annie and Hela created and nurtured to create an ecosystem for connectivity.

"If something's not quite rocking your boat don't complain; do something about it," says Hela.

"Sister Snog is the network we looked for but couldn't find. That's why we now refer to it as a tribe and are not backward in coming forward to say we're actually allergic to the term 'networking'. We promote the idea of connecting," says Annie.

Sister Snog redefines the term *'networking'* so it embraces soft power principles.

Let me rephrase that. Sister Snog recognises that *'networking'* is a word of the past.

Uncomfortable routines are not for them. They've noticed that force-feeding your business cards to every mammal in the room is not the way forward – making connections, on the other hand, is. And a Connectress is the ultimate well-connected woman in business.

The French and Saunders formula

Hela and Annie both emphasise they complement each other. Annie, focused on the systems, putting things in place and making things happen. Yet, in conversation, it is Hela who diligently goes through the listed questions. One by one. With great attention to detail each aspect is analysed and discussed. With Annie, we simply have a chat about the birth of the brand, the past, the present and the future.

They call themselves a double act. Two sides of the same coin. A yin & yang partnership making both halves better and creating one awesome whole. With the two of them at the helm, Sister Snog seduces the mind and logically guides the heart.

Lil & Vi come of age

In February 2017 Sister Snog celebrated their crystal anniversary, bathed in shades of purple. Fifteen years of connecting women in business. Cause for celebration indeed. However, every single Sister Snog event has an element of sparkle and buzz.

The monthly First Friday lunch continues to be the flagship event. Every lunch has a dress code and a creative theme that links to the strategic question that links to the table decoration that links to the copy on the website. That's creative consistency to be impressed by, noticed and learned from.

Look at the visual aspects and assets of the brand. The interchanging lilac and violet spots. The brand symbol is a circle. No hard edges.

Well-defined, kind and powerful.

Sister Snog aligns itself with butterflies. A symbol of transformation. Friday is the favourite day at #snogtowers. Seven is the magic number. With a brand livery that's seven shades of purple: lavender, lilac, wisteria, amethyst, plum, violet and aubergine.

WHY MY BRAND HEROINES?

The creators of Sister Snog have known each other for over a quarter of a century. Two amazing individuals have created one awesome brand. Both hail from a branding background, so of course they understand the power of nurturing a beautiful brand and that strong brands require an equally potent business, with punch to support it and deliver the promise. Sister Snog is a place for member brands to spread their wings and take flight into a colourful world of connectivity. This is a brand created by women, loved by women and driven to new heady heights by women.

Sister Snog is a brand of balance, where style and substance act together in harmony.

Key to Sister Snog's strategy is to fit in and around the many hats of its members and provide a route map to Success City (as Hela calls the ultimate destination for every entrepreneur). Much of this is down to the fact that Sister Snog has created a brand with a real sense of belonging and tight-knit camaraderie between sisters. I guess that is why sisters love Sister Snog.

Sister Snog is like Harley-Davidson, Monty Python and Marmite. You either get it or you don't. And that is why Annie and Hela are my brand heroines.

LESSONS FROM MY CONVERSATION WITH HELA
1. Live the brand you create
2. Finish a task before you start the next one
3. A brand needs guidelines for clarity and consistency
4. Don't be an island – be an archipelago

LESSONS FROM MY CONVERSATION WITH ANNIE
1. Evolution is a must
2. Be remarkable to make your mark
3. You are super lucky if you have found a yin to your yang
4. Go into business with someone who complements you

HELA'S ELEMENTS OF A STRONG BRAND
- CLARITY
- CONSISTENCY
- BEING MEMORABLE
- AIR OF SEDUCTION
- SENSE OF BELONGING
- PIZZAZZ

ANNIE'S ELEMENTS OF A STRONG BRAND
- INTEGRITY
- ALIGNMENT OF VALUES
- DEFINED REACTION: LOVE IT OR HATE IT
- PERSONALITY
- NOT TAKING YOURSELF TOO SERIOUSLY
- BUT BEING SERIOUS ABOUT THE BRAND

INSPIRATION
- Lovemarks.com
- *EVEolution: the Eight Truths of Marketing to Women* by Faith Popcorn & Lys Marigold
- *Purple Cow* by Seth Godin

MOTTO
Hela: *"Anything is possible."* (There should be a pause here to contemplate and appreciate the meaning of these three simple words.)

Annie mentioned a few during our conversation, I noted them all:
- *"Being beautiful has nothing to do with the way you look."*
- *"Don't ignore your gut feeling, it's never wrong."*
- *"Strive for perfection, settle for excellence."*
- Above all: *"Treat people with the same respect you expect to receive from them."*

FIND OUT MORE ABOUT SISTER SNOG
- Visit their website sistersnog.com
- Visit Snog Towers on Twitter twitter.com/snogtowers
- Meet them on Facebook facebook.com/sistersnog/

How serious are you about your brand?

JUSTINA CARMO

Name: Justina Carmo
Speciality: Helping women achieve
Location: London
Reach: National
Key to success: Remembering others without forgetting about yourself
Greatest asset: IP

DREAM LIKE A CHILD

I met Justina at a women-in-business-type networking workshop I ended up attending by accident. Many coaches say there is no such thing as coincidence. In this case, I am prepared to agree with them, as this encounter was of the right-thing-at-the-right-time kind. I wanted to talk to her because, first and foremost, she works with female entrepreneurs who operate outside of their home country. In addition, because she's currently refocusing her business and I am finding it quite fascinating. This was a combination I definitely wanted to investigate further.

A woman, a woman in business

Calm confidence is what I first noticed about Justina. This sensation is not a fleeting one. I get it every time we speak and it is as strong face to face as it is over the phone. Time changes pace during these encounters – in a good way. Suddenly I have time to think, observe without prejudice and analyse constructively. These conversations make me calmer.

Space to be, do, have

Justina builds her brand as a premium product. It's only logical, as she works with people, personal brands. she believes are premium products in the making. She creates an environment that she and her clients are comfortable in.

A journey to success

Her thinking is very consistent. You can clearly see how her knowledge supports her ambition. What do I mean by that? She did not start her career with a view to becoming a coach. Looking for the right thing, she spent a year in Portugal. She spent a few years working as a wine merchant, which gave her the necessary commercial understanding. But that wasn't as satisfying as she had hoped.

There was something new to be discovered and she did not stay lost for long.

The search began: workshops, lectures, events, meetings with people that inspire her. Finally, another coach's suggestion led to a new career. Justina got her qualifications, became a personal coach and never looked back. Today she is still perfecting her craft; she works best with people and organisations at a crossroads – not dissimilar to the ones she had once encountered. She opens their eyes to the possibility of success, helps them make a conscious decision to achieve it and supports them along the way.

Discover, design, achieve

She does it by design. Justina is very aware of her strengths and this is the foundation of her brand. This business brand reiterates the personal values of its creator – her interests, experience and knowledge are at the core of the enterprise.

WHY A BRAND HERO?

The fact that her business mission, which stems from personal experience and vision, is fully aligned with her ambitions makes her one strong brand. It is also the awareness of how her personal and business personalities fit together – it is the way her ambitions and purpose align with education and experience to make the brand even more robust – this is something I admire.

Dream like a child, go and get it.

MY LESSONS FROM THIS CONVERSATION
1. Give yourself credit when it's due

2. Build on your past to have a wider vision of the future
3. Dream like a child and use your adult skills to achieve those dreams

ELEMENTS OF A STRONG BRAND
- CONSISTENCY
- CONFIDENCE
- FOCUS

INSPIRATION
Socrates

MOTTO
"Dream like a child. Use your abilities as an adult to make those dreams come true."

FIND OUT MORE ABOUT JUSTINA
- Visit her website justinacarmo.com
- Like her on Facebook @JustinaCarmoCoaching
- Find her on LinkedIn
- Watch her on YouTube

How confident is your brand?

JULIE CHOO, STRATABILITY

Name of business: Julie Choo, Stratability
Founder: Julie Choo
Years in business: Since January 2016 (Julie, however has been working with C-level executives since early 2000s)
Speciality: Innovation, building capabilities, business strategy, business architecture (especially business model design and operating model optimisation) and technology
Location: London
Reach: International
Key to success: Cash flow & IP
Biggest challenge for businesses: Cash flow
Greatest asset: Curiosity, determination, IP: adding value

LIFE IS A PROTOTYPE: KEEP TESTING, KEEP MORPHING

On her website, Julie introduces herself as a *"techpreneur, author, speaker and strategic advisor focused on education and learning, financial services, innovation, business strategy, business architecture and technology."* She founded Stratability (a boutique learning and consulting practice focused on developing key capabilities) and co-founded Zoomie (an innovative app utilising neuroscience and data science to promote self-awareness and help users drive their careers forward). She is a mentor, a speaker, a writer. These are the roles she undertakes today. She built them on a solid foundation of knowledge and know-how.

She has her own way of doing things.

"There is no point in doing things the traditional way. There are too many people doing things the traditional way. Whether it's your career or anything else, you may as well do it a bit differently." ~ Julie Choo

Julie's personal strategy is not only to be the first one to have that interesting idea, but also to be the one to make things happen. To get that little bit disruptive. To learn, test, assess, improve. To innovate. To do that effectively, she has to know the rules of the discipline she is engaged to disrupt really well. Luckily, Julie enjoys this process of discovery. Always has. In fact, her broad experience thrives when she disrupts – positively – her clients 'projects.

Living innovation

Once upon a time Julie was a software engineer with a career in the financial sector. An employee, with a keen interest in strategy, processes and laws governing the matrix of mergers and acquisitions. She was pushing her career in the direction she was keen on. *"I just kept asking until I got to the right department,"* comments Julie Choo.

Beyond engineering she got a marketing degree, adding product design, international product launch and market assessment to the skill section of her CV. An impressive amalgam. And Julie still keeps learning.

Even when the dot com bubble burst making her job prospects unsatisfyingly bleak when compared to her potential, she created an outlet for her drive and skills through consulting. Exploring banking IT systems, investigating architecture of banking products, architecting tactics of corporate deals. Amongst it all Julie observed her strategy fascination resurfacing. Being a quick learner with such a variety of skills, Julie admits herself bored easily and devising strategies is her way of keeping things interesting. After all strategy is about innovation. Architectures may be transferrable, but each case is different. Julie knows how to combine all the ingredients so her clients grow and trade successfully.

She was once employed by banks and venture capitalists. Today they are among her clients.

Being visible

This transition influenced another shift: in the way Julie markets herself. When you work for someone, especially in the financial services sector, even though you want to be effective and successful, you do not wish to draw attention to yourself. You are often a part of a huge, corporate structure, doing your bit. Being a techpreneur meant the opposite.

Now, as a leader of an organisation, you learn to build an environment in which promoting achievements is a good thing. It is a foundation of organisational culture: uniting and motivating business partners around common values, ideas and practises. Spreading those ideals outside the business helps to build a presence for a brand. Julie knows what she wants her brand to be like: empowering, supportive, innovative. She strategically adds value to services available to her clients and develops comprehensive systems of products. Her book *THE STRATEGY JOURNEY®: Transform your business with agility, accountability & action* explains her process[1] designed to define and achieve victory in business. Stratability utilises Julie's methodology and offers assessments, courses and coaching to help clients become more effective. Stratability aim to *"Accelerate capabilities. Overcome failures. Create success stories."* as they write on their website.

Julie bravely steps into the spotlight by writing blogs, creating products, presenting to clients and nurturing her network. This way, she finds more and more admirers, supporters, business partners and also clients. She builds a strong profile with international outreach.

She leads.

She learns, tests, improves and accelerates. She understands what it means to be a pioneer within your own brand, within your own business.

Courses are selling well, to that level that the first course sold out weeks in advance. Visit stratability.co/ learning-programs for details on the course.

"I moved my business courses to the next level, launching globally in Australia, UK and USA via a digital platform, which I self-learnt how to build in just a few months," comments Julie.

She demonstrates that not only things can be done but if you have the drive and resolve you will organise tools needed to advance

1   These steps are: Mission Model, Business Model, Value Model, Operating Model and Transformation Model. You can find more details on the website www. thestrategyjourney.com/book/strategy-journey

your business. Through courses, her blog, book and speaking engagements Julie empowers clients to unlock their abilities to enable growth. To become more reliable, make actions more effective, spend time efficiently and make the world around them perhaps a little calmer as it fills with a greater amount of happier people. I suppose this is her way of giving back to the society.

"Giving back it is this sort of thing you want to be remembered for."
~ Julie Choo

Beyond Stratability she works hard to give us plenty to get inspired by. During 2016/17 she returned to her roots and refreshed her coding knowledge. This led her to building websites and now she is helping extensively to get more women into STEM.[2] In addition, Julie's passion for data led her to engage with the subject of machine learning and artificial intelligence. She became the MC at the Inaugural European Machine Intelligence and Autonomous Vehicle Summit in Amsterdam in June 2017. That is pretty cool and it means that her brand gains momentum and reaches new audiences.

You can read Julie's writing on the subject of machine and artificial intelligence on her blog thestrategyjourney. com and in her book The Strategy Journey® transform your business with agility, accountability and action.

WHY A BRAND HERO?
To me she seems to be a silver bullet. Fiercely focused. Whatever she is aiming at: product design, engineering, finance... she drills through the subject with unbelievable precision. She does not assume to know everything, she does ask questions: sharp, witty. Julie herself, to me, seems kind and confident...even impressive in that confidence: it is because she means business. And she does it her own way. Having a vision gives her clarity: she understands what is needed and her knowledge tells her where to find it. Being such a multi-skilled person puts Julie in a great position to innovate. She has insight into many fields and can move across them freely, developing comprehensive and well though through solutions. She is a force of positive disruption. It is about that question: if you had a chance to do it all again, would you change anything? If yes, why not change it now. For inspiring that question and facilitating change by giving it a stable architecture, she is my brand hero.

MY LESSONS FROM THIS CONVERSATION
1. Do not wait for someone to give you a chance, make your own

....
2   STEM stands for science, technology, engineering and mathematics.

2. When a good opportunity arrives, be prepared to take it
3. Make yourself visible to attract those chances
4. Be brave in increasing your reach

ELEMENTS OF A STRONG BRAND
- **RESPECT FOR TIME: YOUR OWN, YOUR CLIENTS, YOUR BUSINESS PARTNERS**
- **PLANNING AHEAD**
- **ACTION**

INSPIRATION
- Julie's blog (you can find it on the website thestrategyjourney.com)
- Works of Clayton Christensen, Harvard Business School Professor (no 1 innovation expert in the world)

MOTTO
There are two:
- *"Be a little disruptive."*
- *"Don't be afraid to fail. Just fail fast."*

FIND OUT MORE
- Visit juliechoo.com
- Visit stratability.co
- Tweet @juliechoo
- Read *The Strategy Journey® transform your business with agility, accountability and action* by Julie Choo (due in 2017)

Is your brand positively disruptive?

PATTY CRUZ-FOUCHARD, ORGANISED & SIMPLE

Name of business: Organised & Simple
Founder: Patty Cruz-Fouchard
Years in business: Since 2012
Speciality: Productivity & Organisation Expert
Location: London
Reach: London
Key to success: Love the challenge, you'll find a solution
Biggest challenge for businesses: Getting overwhelmed by the clutter of objects, information and activities
Greatest asset: Energy and positive attitude

PROFESSIONAL LIFE HACKER

A professional organiser is not a title that is intuitively understood this side of the big pond. However, the problem these experts solve, is.

Time dripping through your fingers because there are too many emails to sort through to get to the important ones? Striving to maximise every opportunity and double booking yourself? Aiming to leave in good time, but spending additional five minutes looking for car keys and cutting it very close – again? These are the symptoms of dysfunctionality in our lives. This is what a professional organiser deals with.

Patty Cruz-Fouchard is a pioneer of this discipline.

Method in the madness

There is an Association of Declutterers and Professional Organisers (APDO) here in the UK which has 200 members – so far at least.

Patty, therefore is a pioneer, who promotes this discipline and combines education with practice.

Need: solution

As it is such a niche profession, Patty did not just wake up one morning with a thought of becoming a professional organiser. It is not even the passion for efficient proficiency, but the appreciation for the quality of time that led her to this concept.

She had a corporate career focused on liaising between finance departments and managers. Already, understanding project objectives and efficiency were crucial for her to be successful. Then a new factor appeared in her life – a growing family. Now her problem-solving, analytical skills really came into play. *"If I want to really continue doing this and be good at it I need to spend the least possible amount of time in the office, but still do a good, really good job and not waste time; and also, when I'm at home with my kids, which is very little, I need it to be quality time. So I can't be putting things away all the time. I need to find ways to make my life easier,"* says Patty. She describes herself as being obsessed with finding ways of making things better and not wasting time. And that is hacking!

Shine, without burning out

Worry not, she is not a robot. Patty just wanted to make time to spend time with family, run marathons, have social meetups. She just wasn't willing to give up on anything that really mattered to her. And, she wanted to protect herself from the risk of burning out. So she found a way.

Initially, Patty did not intend to become a professional organiser. After leaving the corporate world she worked with a coach, and it was during her research on the original idea of creating a relocation business that she came across the professional organising industry. As she knew she wanted to work with people, this turned out to be the perfect outlet for her skills.

Space-time continuum

She trained, she qualified and now she practises. The training in this area is US-based and the industry has been recognised there since the 1980s. Patty, in the true spirit of innovation, is personalising it to the UK market.

She works in three areas: space, time and information. It's not about cleaning and making things look pretty, that's just a part of the process. The goal of the exercise is to improve the functionality of the three areas by introducing SYSTEMS and ROUTINES. Patty gives her clients tools to make their lives organised and simple. She gives them the ability to retake control over time.

Ready, set, go

However, to make it work – you have to be ready to make the change. She recognises that people need to feel the need themselves. That is why there are no gift vouchers on her website. Others can't make you want to change, that would be wasting time and that's something she does not do.

A personal approach is key to the success of this venture – both in the approach to the client and in development of the business. Patty understands it very well and the first thing she asks is "What is your vision? Why did you hire me?" Then she introduces bespoke strategies that lead to fulfilling this vision.

When it comes to growing her business, she is an active networker, workshop leader and speaker. This combination works well as she is really a genuinely nice person who is approachable and has this bubbly enthusiasm. I really hope that one day we'll see her in a TV show a la *60 minute makeover*. For now, if you want to work with her, you have to approach her directly.

WHY A BRAND HERO?

I am impressed by Patty's understanding of the market. Modern society breeds generations of overachievers, who are told to rely on themselves and perform. Hence, we accumulate tasks. White noise of information is ubiquitous and we do not want to miss out. Hence, we accumulate data. She brought my attention to the historical context as well. Europe is scarred with wars and conflicts and our grandparents were taught to collect and keep useful items. Then items became cheap and widely available, yet the habit prevailed.

Hence, we accumulate stuff.

She knows that each of us has different reasons for behaving the way we do. She makes a point of discovering our stories and giving us tools to make the following chapters even more impressive. Making pens and paper easy to find when we need them may also be a part of the process!

That is why Patty is my brand hero.

MY LESSONS FROM THIS CONVERSATION
1. Your business is about people
2. The client needs to be ready to take action to make the most of the solution
3. Choose your priorities and find an expert to help you with everything else

ELEMENTS OF A STRONG BRAND
- CLARITY
- SPACE TO GROW
- VISION
- PERSONAL STORY
- & MAKING A DIFFERENCE TO PEOPLE'S LIVES

INSPIRATION
Kim Kiyosaki, for her approach to women's financial education

MOTTO
"Don't limit yourself, anything is possible"

FIND OUT MORE
- Visit the website organisedandsimple.com
- Follow them on Twitter: @OrganisedPatty
- Watch them on YouTube: Organisedandsimple
- Find Patty on LinkedIn: linkedin.com/in/pattycruzfouchard
- Discover them on Facebook: facebook.com/Organisedsimple

How is your brand making a difference to people's lives?

EMMA LOUISE DAVIDSON, AFFINITY CAPITAL

Name of business: Affinity Capital
Founder: Emma Louise Davidson
Years in business: Since October 2011
Speciality: Structured investments and derivatives
Location: London
Key to success: Find a space to be yourself in business
Biggest challenge for businesses: Finding a space to be yourself in business
Greatest asset: Ability to develop partnerships

SHE'S A LADY

She could be a business coach, but she prefers to be a quiet achiever. I am constantly amazed by her success, but not surprised. Emma's not a person who puts herself on a pedestal. She feels more comfortable behind the scenes, making sure all is set and ready for when her clients need to step on the stage. But my advice would be to look her up and keep an eye on how she develops her brand. She is one wise lady. Humble, incredibly polite and super-smart.

"Whatever choices we make, they have an impact. But the decisions don't have to be permanent." ~ Emma Louise Davidson

I find safety in this thought. For a long time I myself have been afraid of setting goals for myself. All because I was anxious my plans would turn out to be the wrong ones. Conversation with Emma made me realise (and it really was like an epiphany – in Costa Coffee, of all places) that business decisions you make now have the biggest impact on 'the now'. Circumstances change, that's a given – decisions, therefore, can change too, so don't be afraid to make them.

"It's not easy to decide. But you have to be flexible and grow. You are never done as a business." ~ Emma Louise Davidson

She chose what is traditionally perceived to be a cold, tough environment – finance. This industry is not only dominated by men, but men who are going in for the kill. Yet, she thrives in it, without losing her femininity and kindness. What is more, she made it her business. Affinity Capital is in perfect alignment with Emma's personality.

She invests in partnerships with her clients and gets to know them, and allows them to get to know her. She is not aggressive or intimidating. She does not have to be. It is a choice to develop relationships organically, based on true understanding of the client. By getting rid of assumptions, she makes room for partnerships.

It is a brave move. But she is a professional, she knows what she's doing. And she has given herself the permission to do it her own way.

When most of us contemplate the world of finance and managing multimillion pound investments, we think about faceless corporate structures. Emma's living proof that it's good to question stuff, and she's made a conscious decision not to go that way. It takes time to realise you do not have to do everything in your business and to allow yourself not to do everything. *"It frees up your time to focus on what you know best,"* says Emma. *"I sometimes think that I could scale up, take on more clients. But then I remind myself I do not want this. I am very much aware that this is a lifestyle business and I want to keep it that way. I want to enjoy it and have time,"* she continues.

It is a man's world

While male egos hide behind corporate policies, Emma makes a bold move to show her face. She invests in her online profile, which will give you the same impression of values as her website and book. Affinity Capital's business brand is being developed on solid foundations of the strong personal brands of its leaders.

WHY A BRAND HERO?
Emma focuses her efforts on one face, one image, one set of values – the ones that are true to her. It's not only easier that way, but

it projects a stronger image as well. Affinity Capital is doing very well. Emma is planning to build a business in Australia. I have every confidence it is going to be equally successful. I will be impressed, but not surprised. That is why she is my hero.

MY LESSONS FROM THIS CONVERSATION

1. Choosing your place enables you to focus on what you're good at
2. Watch others and learn in order to develop confidence to be yourself
3. It does not make sense to have a business face and a personal face – you'll get found out

ELEMENTS OF A STRONG BRAND
- HAVING A HUMAN FACE
- ALLOWING YOURSELF TO LEARN & GROW
- BEING HERE AND NOW

INSPIRATION
Sheryl Sandberg, for the way she challenges women, and Warren Buffett, for showing that philanthropy is very much a thing of today.

FIND OUT MORE
- Visit their website affinitycapital.co.uk
- Keep up to date with Emma on Twitter @AffinityCapital
- LinkedIn: find Emma Louise Davidson

What is the focus of your brand?

CHRIS DOCHERTY & STEVE GUNNELL, FISTFUL OF SPICE

Name of business: Fistful of Spice
Founders: Chris Docherty & Steve Gunnell
Years in business: Since 2014
Speciality: Artisan chilli products
Location: Milton Keynes
Reach: National
Key to success: Respect the ingredients (of the business, of the products, of the community)
Biggest challenge for businesses: Dilution
Greatest asset: They say *"product and brand"*, I say: Chris's and Steve's philosophy to partnership and product

SOME LIKE IT HOT

What a pleasure it has been to meet Chris and Steve and to talk to them. I met them at the Great Wild Food and Chilli Fair in Heybridge, Maldon.

Their name stood out. The visual identity was intriguing. And the guys behind the stand were smiling. They are really the nicest people you could have met.

We started talking. My first impression was that I am looking at the Ben & Jerry of spice. Perhaps. But, when I got to talk to them a little longer I knew they are unlike anyone else. Chris and Steve are creating a brand of their own.

Soon, if it's not happening already, others will want to be like them.

Positioning – defined

In addition, they agreed early on that they are not going to position themselves on the jokey end of the chilli brand spectrum. They analysed the market and themselves, and defined a place they want to be in: artisan.

They are making a stand, creating a chilli philosophy, developing an experience beyond sauces. The way I see it, they represent a certain school of culinary thinking. Yes, there's a punch (hence the fist in the logo). But it's not designed to knock you down, but to enlighten. Fistful of Spice blows your socks off in order to open your mind to more possibilities of how chilli can enrich your senses. Talking to the brains behind the brand made me realise that what they are creating is an experience and has the makings of a culture. Perhaps even a cult.

Think about the Converse – quality in itself; a brand widely recognised and understood as a symbol of a certain state of mind.

Ground rules

They grow it slowly, walking steadily before they will run. I don't think it will take long for them to pick up a pace though. Ingredients are there and the mixture is potent. All it needs is a few more outlets and perhaps a stronger online presence; but it will come, I am sure. These guys love their craft but they mean business. They know where they want to go – and they are also determined to remember where it all began.

First and foremost, they are friends.

"We remember that the friendship was there first."
~ Chris Docherty & Steve Gunnell

It takes precedence over any creative differences they may have. This clarity of rules and honesty towards each other is what I think may keep them from the spectacular split-ups of the likes of Fleetwood Mac.

Additional ingredients

Then, they experiment. Remember *MythBusters*? This is how I imagine Chris & Steve in their kitchen: safety goggles, white coats, blue gloves. Testing formulae for new chilli + [ingredient x] permutations. Some combinations take longer to perfect than others; but, however painful the process may be, they persevere. They suffer, so we don't have to. Don't pity them too much because they know that every now and then a miracle happens – they stumble upon something that bewitches the mind, ensnares the senses.

Honesty is the basis of their recipes

They only sell what they would buy themselves. Even more importantly, they only sell what they would eat themselves. One thing is certain – they never compromise on taste and flavour. Understanding that the product is only as good as its ingredients is ubiquitous. Yet, we somehow allowed them to be diluted in all the E-preservatives and colourants... but I'm digressing.

Artisan is the key word here. The duo are already working on diversifying within their concept – oils, barbecue sets, flavour boosters. They want to grow the business – and no doubt, they will. The products are gradually becoming more accessible, but the way this brand is evolving – and what I think is excellent about it – it's going to be a brand you want to reach out for. Think delicatessen, appreciation, experience.

The approach of some chilli-product manufacturers can be summed up with a quote: "Our orders are to make sure he does not die...but also to make sure he regrets the day he was born."
That is a quote from "A Fistful of Dollars", a 1964 spaghetti western directed by Sergio Leone.

Add relationship with local farmers, knowledge of how to choose and combine flavours, funky identity... and you get one tasteful brand.

With Fistful of Spice, flavour beats Scovilles.

WHY A BRAND HERO?

They are memorable, straightforward and genuinely enjoyable to talk to. Their enthusiasm towards their brand and their obvious expertise was actually uplifting, if that makes sense. I have to admit I am not a chilli person. People have told me that different peppers have different flavours – sweet, sour, earthy... so they said. To me there used to be one flavour: pain. But looking at Fistful of Spice, I believe them. There is flavour. A hotness, yes, but it serves a purpose. I want to try it. It is because these guys are so awesome, I am willing to put my preconceptions away and actually dive in. Well, taste a little bit of the Mango Chilli. On a cracker. With a glass of milk within reach, just in case. But I'm in!

Beyond that, they are creating a community. They encourage others to share their uses of the Fistful of Spice range. They truly live their chilli concept. And long may they live.

MY LESSONS FROM THIS CONVERSATION
1. Sort out your priorities, this will help you develop your business and create stronger products
2. Love what you do, do what you love
3. Be true to yourself and the rest will flow

ELEMENTS OF A STRONG BRAND
- ENTHUSIASM
- AUTHENTICITY
- DRIVE

INSPIRATION
Fistful of Spice recommend you check out Brew Dog UK, for their products, business model and visual side of the brand are equally amazing. If you like them, look up citylicious.net as well.

MOTTO
An ethos more than a motto: *"quality + balance = we wouldn't sell it if we wouldn't eat it"*

FIND OUT MORE
- Visit their website and online shop fistfulofspice.co.uk
- Follow them on Twitter @fistfulofspice
- Find them on Facebook at facebook.com/fistfulofspice

What is your brand's special recipe?

RAFAEL DOS SANTOS, DIGITAL ENTREPRENEUR ACADEMY

Name of business: Digital Entrepreneur Academy
Founder: Rafael dos Santos
Years in business: 14
Speciality: Helping entrepreneurs turn their expertise into online courses
Location: London
Reach: National
Key to success: Network of contacts
Biggest challenge for businesses: To remain yourself, whether on stage or during a face-to-face meeting
Greatest asset: Ability to connect people

MAKING IT HAPPEN

Ten years ago, Rafael did not even speak English. Today we meet in the heart of London, at the Institute of Directors (IOD), to talk about his brand. Impressive progression by any account, and one we can all learn from.

The tube is on strike and traffic is abysmal. I wait for him in the lobby of the IOD. When he arrives he's all smiles, despite the challenges of the commute. We go in for a coffee and, even though our meeting had to be reduced to half an hour (his diary is unforgiving, despite the challenges of the day), we manage to cover essential matters of branding and approach to business.

We have stayed in contact and cooperated on his Migrant Business Accelerator since, so, despite the short meeting, I believe I am in a position to give you an account of what kind of a brand Rafael dos Santos represents.

Here we go.

American business style
British endurance
Brazilian personality

Rafael is an experienced entrepreneur. He's built businesses with international reach, he has known success as well as failure and still his enthusiasm is unrivalled. That is what, in my eyes, makes him a true entrepreneur.

I suppose he can have a Marmite effect on people as he has a vibrant, strong personality, but he is deadly serious about business. He is a larger-than-life personality and chose London to be his home. Having observed him online – well, his business profile – and then meeting him in person, I've come to the conclusion that he combines Brazilian approach to celebration, American approach to money and British approach to relationships. Let me explain.

The beginnings were tough. Brazil is not all carnival and bullying is a social problem of that environment, so much so that by the time he reached his 18th birthday, Rafael was determined to leave. He was about to turn 21 when he moved to the UK. Even though he used to work for Microsoft as an analyst, on British soil, due to his lack of English, he started in the kitchens.

Then, by improving his English he improved his language skills, and that opened up job opportunities. Eventually he became a teaching assistant and then moved on to sales for big fashion brands. His interpersonal skills landed him a job for Chanel and he became the best in the area. The next step was to become a property magnate.

He was very successful in what he did, yet the way of the managers, or the way that they tried to approach him, did not really click with the strategies he was implementing to achieve success. And his phone was ringing all the time, because he was running his own rental business simultaneously. Basically, he used to get fired from jobs for being an entrepreneur. The latter overtook the requirements of the 9 to 5.

Influence beyond borders

He grew his properties from one to 50, with 15 employees. This, however, made him realise that his selling talent was not being utilised to the full. Hence, the new venture, Migrant Business Accelerator and mi-HUB being the flagships.

He gels American business style with British strategies and uses his unique background to help other entrepreneurs learn how to pitch their ideas, launch partnerships, and get funding.

Rafael teaches people how to bring the two worlds together: the heritage, your origins, where you come from and the reality of land you wish to build your success into. He does it himself – that is why he is the right person to do it. He's not theorising, he is sharing his experience.

Since our conversation he has launched the Migrant Business Accelerator programme under the banner of social enterprise This Foreigner Can – check it out. Irrespective of your background it is worth following and observing how this brand comes to life and what it achieves. His new venture is the Digital Entrepreneurs Academy (go to www. digitalentrepreneurs. academy) where he helps entrepreneurs turn their expertise into online courses.

His programme is like his personality; vibrant, proactive, open to opportunities and very down to earth. Especially when choosing feasible solutions and systems that can support them. He is the best ambassador of the brand; the atmosphere Rafael creates around himself and the type of people he chooses to cooperate with support his core values. Kudos.

He does not want to stop there. Helping migrant entrepreneurs support the British economy is just the first step. Rafael also has ideas on how to open our youth to entrepreneurship and he plans to create a one-day workshop for 11–17-year-olds at their schools, when they can get to grips with challenges from creating a marketable idea to figuring out distribution channels.

Quicksilver

Rafael is such an active person. He says it is hard for him to focus on any one task for a long time; I suppose managing all those ideas at once is a trick to making things happen. And when he does, they vibrate with enthusiasm and possibility, like he himself so often does. It seems that all Rafael's journeys led to this point – This Foreigner Can, career-wise, is his favourite thing to do. It also inspires other entrepreneurs – to donate their time and share their knowledge, or to take part in the programme and shape up. If you get a chance to attend one of his conferences, do; it will be time well invested.

WHY A BRAND HERO?

Rafael refuses to let the word 'migrant' be used as a derogatory term. He proves it can be an advantage, he makes it an advantage. He uses it as a reason to work harder, do better and achieve more. He redefines it as a term describing adventurers: resilient and resourceful people who want to make lives better for themselves and others. It does not mean that there are no pitfalls in this life. There are dark days in the lives of every entrepreneur. I guess if you are sensitive enough to notice an area for improvement and you decide to do something about it, you are buying yourself an emotional rollercoaster with life-changing highs and exasperating lows. Having said that, Rafael continues the ride, and he is making each ride the best experience yet, in his own, unmistakable style. For that, he is my brand hero.

MY LESSONS FROM THIS CONVERSATION

1. Grab the opportunities as they come along
2. Be realistic and know when to give up and move on
3. Work hard and do not be embarrassed by the pitfalls; learn from them and do all you can to perform better next time

ELEMENTS OF A STRONG BRAND

- **FEELING STRONGLY ABOUT WHAT YOU STAND FOR**
- **FINDING PARTNERSHIPS THAT SUPPORT YOUR QUEST**
- **INSPIRING A FOLLOWING**

INSPIRATION

- *The Psychology of Selling* by Brian Tracy
- Deborah Meaden
- Peter Jones
- James Caan
- Darshana Ubl
- Marcus Ubl

MOTTO

"Nothing happens if you stay at home, but don't try to run before you learn how to walk."

FIND OUT MORE

- His personal website rafaeldossantos.com
- Visit Digital Entrepreneurs Academy: www.digitalentrepreneurs.academy
- You can also read his book Moving Abroad One Step at a Time at rafaeldossantos.com/book/

What kind of partnerships would support your brand?

KATHY ENNIS, LITTLEPIGGY ASSOCIATES LTD

Name of business: Kathy Ennis, LittlePiggy Associates Ltd
Founder: Kathy Ennis
Years in business: Since 2001
Speciality: Personal branding and visual communication (tied up in Kathy's Plan – Brand – Market approach)
Location: London
Reach: National, focused on South East
Key to success: Learning, testing and doing more of the stuff that works
Biggest challenge for businesses: Implementation
Greatest asset: Ability to search for answers

51271[1]

THE WORLD OF BUSINESS NEEDS MORE LIBRARIANS

I met Kathy when she was delivering a presentation on personal branding in email marketing. Her image makes it easy to recall that "she was the one who delivered it".

She did make an impact – with her personal branding. The effect was that I wanted to know more about her business, her plans and how I could possibly be of use. We set up a follow up 1-2-1 meeting to do just that.

This is exactly what each brand hopes for when they meet their

....

1   Kathy's favourite number – the number of times James Dyson did not invent his famous hoover; had he given up at attempt no. 10, he may have been known just for the improved barrel, or not even known as an inventor at all.

peers or prospective clients at an event.

Kathy Ennis works with microbusinesses and over-50s who consider creating a business for the first time. She champions business education, development and self-awareness – she helps people discover whether business is their route to happiness. If it is, she helps them identify and leverage their personal brand within it.

However, she has not always been a personal brand expert. This was not a career she dreamed of doing at school. She is quite frank about this: *"When I left school I had no idea what I wanted to do."* She got a degree in History of Film only to hit months of unemployment. Then she became a library assistant and things started falling into place. Professional development, the ability to search for information and to find out what people are really looking for – all got embedded into her professional self. But it was not *it* – not yet. Only years later, when her husband presented her with colour analysis for a birthday, did she really come into her own. This one consultation changed the way she viewed herself.

Colour yourself beautiful

"It was not about fashion, but about what am I saying if I put this on," says Kathy. This experience sparked an interest in visual communication and impression management, which triggered her evolution into a personal branding professional. Her goal is to share this feeling of confidence with others in business. And this awareness is crucial, especially in the world of microbusiness, where – in order to survive in the market – people need to claim ownership of themselves.

Entrepreneurship is a mindset

"We need to give young people and business the option to discover what they want. And fail. Then explain why it went wrong. This is the only way to learn," Kathy explains. It's not only about having to create a business; if you really want to start a new venture, you need to do it for the right reasons. If you try it and decide you actually want to get back into employment, because what you really want is a sense of security, that's OK. You are not a lesser person because of it. This situation has nothing to do with failure.

Learn, test, improve, repeat. But when you have a passion and want to turn it into a business and you have never done that before, you will do well to remember this quote from Kathy: *"You know your stuff. What you do not know is business."* Do not let that stop you, just learn as much as you can and be prepared to shift the focus from your art to promoting it. Create assets and then focus on how to distribute them to your audience.

It' is easier if you develop yourself as a brand.

To become a brand, you need to find your true motivation and build on it. Then you'll be able to create and project the right image.

Be a good brand, if you can. If you are motivated by money, that is OK. Just remember that entrepreneurs are these strange people at the forefront of business development who pay themselves last. Kathy and I agree that flogging goods perhaps brings faster return on investment (ROI), but in reality there is only so much you can make this way. However, when you are a brand, a business on a mission, the warm-up may take longer, but ultimately it leads to better and greater things – for you and for your clients; it brings better value to all.

WHY A BRAND HERO?

She is an example of how effective having a memorable personal brand can be. She helps people assess whether business is the right route for them as many lifestyle businesses are being created not out of choice, but necessity, due to retirement or redundancy. But when they decide *yes*, she gives them the tools and support to grow.

Yes, aspiring entrepreneurs can find a plethora of business information and *how-tos* online. Perhaps even too much. Choosing the right information takes time – and then there is the little matter of implementation.

In the PG (pre-Google) era, libraries were the hubs of information. Even though each housed a finite number of volumes, each had an advantage over Google today – a librarian, a person who willingly gave advice on implementation and sometimes even supervised the progress. Kathy Ennis is a modern-day business librarian.

MY LESSONS FROM THIS CONVERSATION

1. Best lessons come from situations when things don't go according to the plan, so do not let them pass unobserved
2. Not everyone has to go into business; it's OK to want to have a job, as long as it makes you happy
3. Business can be fun, but people can make a lot of hard work for themselves, so systemise, productise and delegate

ELEMENTS OF A STRONG BRAND

- ### CONSISTENCY WITH THE PERSONAL BRAND OF ITS CREATOR
- ### LEARNING FROM MISTAKES
- ### MISSION

INSPIRATION

- Blink by Malcolm Gladwell (a great how-to book for the service-based business, one of the few that is not focused on production and manufacturing)
- Grow Your Service Firm by Robert Craven

MOTTO

"It pays to plan ahead. It wasn't raining when Noah built the ark!"

FIND OUT MORE

- Visit Kathy's website littlepiggy.ltd
- LinkedIn profile /in/kathyennis
- Facebook page LittlePiggyUK
- ...and Twitter @kathyennis

What do you consider the greatest value of your brand? What do your clients see as the greatest value of your brand?

CLAUDIA FALLAH, CLAUDIA FALLAH COSMECEUTICALS

Name of business: Claudia Fallah Cosmeceuticals
Founder: Claudia Fallah
Years in business: Since 1999
Speciality: Cosmeceuticals (cosmetics engineered to have medicinal benefits)
Location: London
Reach: International
Key to success: Determination in being, and doing, the best you can
Biggest challenge for businesses: Focus
Greatest asset: Determination and knowledge

THE PURSUIT OF EXCELLENCE

Claudia believes in good outcomes. This was my first impression of her. We met at a networking dinner and what I remember most is her smile and positive curiosity. She is a type of person you want to make time to talk to. The conversation flows, easily. Claudia is focused, precise and has a witty sense of humour. She appreciates the value of time. She is also very brave. Uncompromising in pursuit of excellence. She builds her brand on those features.

To be at the heart of the industry

Claudia moved from Germany to the UK in the mid nineties to be at the heart of the industry. To a place with the biggest possibilities and equally matched challenges for any new business. Her great challenge was to make it in the beauty industry. Yet, this is where she wanted to be. London. And she was determined.

When you arrive in a new place with not much more than the clothes on your back you just have to make it.

You make a decision to make it.

A conscious decision not to go back. Of course, you do your best to prepare yourself in terms of knowledge, but you make that choice to take just one direction: onwards.

You choose not to create a backup plan to fall back on.

You choose to go on.

If you are going to make it you may as well make it big

In choosing her challenges, Claudia never holds back. She always goes for the big ones. It is a part of her personality. It became a part of her personality when she overcame a challenge of dealing with problematic skin.

Having difficulties with your own skin is hardship enough. People should not also suffer when trying to deal with it. Therefore, having been appalled by the quality of service she once received in a beauty clinic, Claudia decided that no one should ever feel disappointed with the level of professionalism at such a place. In addition, cosmeceuticals for delicate, traumatised skin should not be near-impossible to get. Not while she had something to say about it.

Claudia developed a professional relationship with a chemist to help her develop her own formulations that followed another simple, yet challenging rule: to use what is needed, nothing else.

Each ingredient needs to have a purpose. Embellishments, just for the sake of adding something, are to be prohibited. It is a good rule. A hard one to follow sometimes, though: when it comes to both finding such pure products on the store shelves and developing business. Claudia implements this rule in both.

Getting rid of distractions

The brand gains momentum and this can be a tricky stage. Claudia found a way to stay true to her own nature amidst the growing buzz. The cosmeceuticals that had initially been developed for use in her own clinic are now present in a few selected London boutiques. The interest grows organically and the distribution channel swells nicely.

She is as honest as the ingredients she decides to use in her products. She is an advocate of setting clear boundaries and requirements, especially when dealing with suppliers and your team. This means being open, kind and honest about what you are after.

Conversation with Claudia is a lesson in how not to allow setbacks undermine your belief in the positive outcome. Staying true to the formula allowed Claudia to achieve so much and she keeps achieving.

Believe there is a way and find people that can help you achieve it. There are people who will want to help you out.

The brand is getting ready to blossom.

WHY A BRAND HERO?
She focuses on what works. It is as simple as it is challenging.

When thinking about new formulations, Claudia believes all the power we need to make a product work with our skin is there, in nature, already. She seeks out ingredients that have that ability and works hard to combine them in a way that does not diminish it.

When it comes to creating a strong brand, it is all there in your nature, too.

The trick is to get rid of the distractions. Claudia did it by sticking to her own formula: in the media, in her products, when you meet her, you see the true face of the brand, and that makes it so much easier to recognise and admire the value of what the brand offers.

MY LESSONS FROM THIS CONVERSATION
1. Focus on what your brand is truly about and be faithful to your nature
2. Identify elements that obstruct your clarity and get rid of them
3. Be brave and act: you are not alone in this, even as a solopreneur

ELEMENTS OF A STRONG BRAND
- CLARITY
- FOCUS

- RELIABILITY
- PASSION
- FORMULA TO MAKE IT WORK

INSPIRATION
Biography of Walt Disney, as a lesson in how to overcome obstacles and keep fulfilling your vision.

MOTTO
"Do not let fear stop you."

FIND OUT MORE
- Visit claudiafallah.co.uk
- Look them up on Facebook @Claudia.Fallah.Cosmeceuticals.Limited
- Follow them on Twitter @ClaudiaFallah
- Find them on Instagram claudiafallah and use #consultclaudia
- Add them on Google+ +ClaudiafallahUkskincare

What is your challenge of choice?

SONIA GILL, HEADS UP

Name of business: Heads Up
Founder: Sonia Gill
Years in business: Since 2010
Speciality: Head teacher training and school management
Location: London
Reach: National
Key to success: Creating a high-performing culture
Biggest challenge for businesses: Clarity on mission
Greatest asset: IP

UP YOUR ANTE

We first met at a business course and Sonia stood out of the crowd due to the clarity and passion of her vision: making schools outstanding. It's an honourable quest and the subject alone was intriguing enough for me to interview her. But there are other contributing factors as well.

She is all engagement, enthusiasm, energy, fast pace and thought; an exhilarating mixture that led her to win the pitching competition. She came first out of 50. She knows her subject, she knows her business and she is the nicest. One of the kindest women on a mission you will ever meet.

We sit down in a café at the ground-floor central London office and chat about the Heads Up brand.

Talk the talk, rock the walk

A psychologist and a teacher herself, she is on a mission to make schools places where true learning happens, not only education. Sonia does that by working with the school, and with Heads Up they learn how to go through difficult conversations, define their vision and ignite their spirit. Heads Up helps these organisations speak with one voice, showing their pupils the powers of teamwork, unity and vision. She can do that, because she does it herself.

She did that even in her previous professional life, when she developed teams for John Lewis. So, she says, the transition into education was an organic one.

"I just think about where I can add value. Where's the market and the opportunity? If I am to do something, I want it to be something I enjoy doing" ~ Sonia Gill

Knowledge → expertise → new market, that seems to be the path that led to starting this brand.

In order to be able to communicate her brand with clarity, Sonia joined a business development course and wrote a book. That optimised her IP.

For Heads Up, it comes down to the ability to create a culture that excites people within it. She works with heads and leadership teams and it cascades through to the school and students. It is a brand whose mission is to show their clients strategies of how to become their better and best selves. And then pass it on.

She is there to rearrange the pieces so that they can withstand the pressure. With the appreciation of the talent already in school, analysing their strengths and making them realise where they can do better – but she does it in a way so they can really better themselves. It is not teaching them but creating an environment in which the educators truly learn and want to become outstanding beyond Ofsted's requirements.

One thing she refuses to accept is stagnation. The *good enough* attitude does not compute with Sonia, and her brand does not believe in situations that cannot be improved, as long as there is a will to make that change. This is achieved by identifying and clarifying the schools' goals, and supporting them on the way. It is activating teams and backing them up during the process.

A particular brand

I would say that she identifies brands of schools Heads Up works with and helps them develop goals based on that.

The great thing is they are not waiting for the legislation to change but making that improvement regardless.

It is a challenging environment, filled with pressure and stress; wanting to be outstanding can easily be overshadowed by the everyday challenges of a head teacher. When good is all you need to pass... She refuses to agree to that level. 'Outstanding' can be achieved and that is what she is and helps others aim for.

WHY A BRAND HERO?

Heads Up looks at what else is possible within their sector. Good enough is not good enough for them and their excellent example shows other organisations how to up their ante.

The book, their process, their website – all expressions of the brand are filled with their passion, but it is clear that their service is focused on the needs of the client. Each course is moulded to fit the school.

Educating educators is one hell of a challenge. Heads Up, it's a brave new world. Creating culture where improvement is achievable; analysing areas for improvement is a virtue that leads to a better future and challenges the mediocre status quo.

Heads Up fills me with hope, as the fact that they thrive in the market means our schools are getting better and better. That there is not only room for improvement, but action towards that as well.

MY LESSONS FROM THIS CONVERSATION

1. Finding areas that need improving does not mean you failed, it means you can do better
2. It is easy to lose distance towards your own business; if you can, get an external expert to help you get an unbiased opinion about the state of affairs
3. Every assessment is an opportunity to show how good you are at what you do and to find out how much better you can get

ELEMENTS OF A STRONG BRAND
- CLARITY OF VISION
- ENGAGING MISSION
- COMMITMENT

MOTTO
"Outstanding leadership creates outstanding schools"

FIND OUT MORE
- Visit their website ukheadsup.com
- Read the book *Journey to Outstanding* (you can find it on amazon. co.uk/JourneyOutstanding-Sonia-Gill/)
- Watch them on YouTube (you can look for Sonia Gill Heads Up or type this address: youtube.com/channel/ UCr3QCVGDRGrsb6QYvooJwjg
- Find Sonia on LinkedIn (look for Sonia Gill)

What did you learn about your brand? What does your brand teach others?

GINA HARDY, GINA HARDY YOGA

Name of business: Gina Hardy Yoga
Founder: Gina Hardy
Years in business: Since 2008 (although Gina has been practising yoga for over 20 years)
Speciality: Yoga for everyday people
Location: Surrey
Reach: International
Key to success: Stopping for long enough to find your essence (*"The elixir of life happens in the stillness"* ~ Gina Hardy)
Biggest challenge for businesses: Finding yourself
Greatest asset: Being able to choose your own clients

APOSTLE OF BEAUTY

She's one of the entrepreneurs who is quite active on social media and I'd been following Gina's online presence for quite some time before approaching her. Her messages caught my eye as they have always been, and still are, candid and wholesome. Gina's thing is yoga, and she has a very elegant manner in building a profile for herself and her business.

She's not a militant yogini and appreciates that yoga may not be for everyone, yet she shows it from an angle that encourages you to try, if you want to and when you are ready. Her manner is caring and wholesome. I wanted to talk to her about how she became that way and so we arrange a Skype conversation for a Wednesday morning in July. She is housesitting for a friend and behind her, I see a majestic tree, whose leaves are letting in glimmering rays of sun. Quite a fitting backdrop for a talk about living your life in yoga.

Gina started looking into yoga, as it often happens, to counterbalance stresses of personal and corporate life.

In the beginning, yoga wasn't a passion, simply a place of deep comfort and peace. However, with time, affinity to that space grew, so she trained to become a teacher.

"Your body is your greatest gift, beyond anyone or anything, and yoga gives me the opportunity of teaching you that beauty, reconnecting you to that beauty." ~ Gina Hardy

In her previous professional life, she worked in aviation, in project development, and it was always about communication; then as a relationship coach, and, in a manner of speaking, she still is in that business. Through yoga she is coaching her students to better the relationship they have with their bodies, with themselves. Communicating with their bodies.

In the future she wants to have more retreats, in soothing locations all over the world. She plans to continue working with small groups, 10 to 12 pupils at once. She prefers it that way as it allows her to stay connected and continue her very engaged approach to teaching. Also, teaching 1-2-1 plays a big part in her brand, which is now a lifestyle, but she also has international business, with retreats in Spain and Greece, and in the future in Mexico as well.

What does success look like? Being able to choose your clients.

"I get to choose my clients. Within the first conversation I can tell if they are actually committed enough to do the work necessary to gain the enormous benefits from doing yoga and I think it's important not to say YES to every client if you feel it's not going to be a good partnership for change." ~ Gina Hardy

It can only happen if you deliver a service of sufficient quality.

"I need to be developing my life and my client's life; it has to be mutually beneficial. In order to be at your best you've got to want to. You've got to want to go 'oh my, this client is amazing' and then they get their best." ~ Gina Hardy

It is almost ironic; you get more clients when you get to choose them – by becoming exclusive to a certain extent, you get better results, the process is more pleasurable. By not being everything to everyone you give yourself a much better chance of being really good at something and finding those someones who will truly benefit from it and appreciate the process.

And people are leaning much more towards a conscious world – making choices, deciding what they are comfortable with and being clear in communicating it. Gina's yoga – *"yoga for everyday people"* – is a part of that environment. She is part of that mindset herself and that is why she can serve her clients so beautifully.

It's yoga beyond fitness. Fitness with a soul. A life companion, as Gina calls it. Her own brand, through and through.

WHY A BRAND HERO?

The story of a corporate worker looking for a new career is not a unique one. However, the way Gina's story unfolds - is unique. I am fascinated by the way pieces of her expertise and approach flow into place. As if they were simply reaching their pre-designed destination. They build a story of a brand that is warm, professional and truthful.

Gina does not teach yoga for the sake of perfecting postures and stretching. Her quest is to reawaken people's communion with their beauty, and yoga represents a means to an end.

She is her brand

She is not scared to make sure her clients are ready to work with her. That way she makes sure they can truly benefit from the service. She is focused on the individual and adamant that quality of service is to be true to her own values – the delivery, the location, the style of yoga itself. Gina makes sure her brand, her personal brand, is visible through every aspect of her business.

One more thing – Gina's clients are at the centre of her activities. Reawakening their beauty is at the core. She is brave enough to do it while not forgetting about herself, enabling her to keep the quality at such a high level. This beauty that Gina promotes and the way she does it, so beautifully human, is truly inspiring, and that is why she is my brand hero.

MY LESSONS FROM THIS CONVERSATION
1. Make time for keeping still
2. It's OK to make a choice
3. You can be a fascinating brand even if you do not think "you are born yet"; some of the most beautiful brands think about themselves as brands in the making

ELEMENTS OF A STRONG BRAND
- **BEING TRUE TO ITS AUTHENTIC ESSENCE IN ALL ITS ACTIVITIES**
- **FOCUSING ON CLIENTS, AT THE SAME TIME NOT FORGETTING ABOUT ITSELF**

"Whe you are truly open, from a divine place, you are an absolute magnet to the world because you are coming from a heart-centred place, almost out of the way of your personality; somehow what you create, connects." ~ Gina Hardy

INSPIRATION
- Danielle Marchant for her wisdom
- Holly Helt from Chiki Tea for her spirit
- Elspeth Mclean (Mandala Stones) for her creations
- Rachel Brathen, yoga – for the true essence of her teaching she makes visible through her brand

MOTTO
"Live. Learn. Love. And pay it forward."

FIND OUT MORE
- Visit her website ginahardy.co.uk (Gina Hardy teaches hatha yoga, yin yoga and restorative yoga)
- Find her on Facebook facebook.com/gina.hardy.
- Follow on Twitter @GinaHardy1
- Watch on YouTube GinaHardyYoga
- Connect with Gina on LinkedIn
- ...and observe on Instagraminstagram.com/yogag

Who do you choose as your clients?

MARIANNE HARTLEY, HARTLEY & SOUL

Name of business: Hartley & Soul
Founder: Marianne Hartley
Years in business: Since June 2013
Speciality: Healing design
Location: London and Basel
Reach: International
Key to success: Being your true self and enjoying what you do
Biggest challenge for businesses: Disconnection
Greatest asset: Connecting to the heart

MANDALA FOR THE MODERN WORLD

We have known each other online longer than we have in person. However, in whichever universe I meet Marianne, we effortlessly pick up where we left off. She divides her time between London and Basel; however, she is a 100% awesome designer and it's the soul behind the designs we are going to talk about.

This time we meet face to face, for the second time, in a quirky café on Old Street – Look Mum No Hands. It is Wednesday, 9am, Marianne finishes her bowl of granola and I am waiting for my smoothie. We begin.

You are the starting point

Being a designer is one thing. Being a designer creating projects that make you pause for a second and appreciate their beauty, is another. Marianne is the latter type of a creator. What fascinates me is that she manages to produce this exquisiteness not only for her clients, but for her own brand as well.

Those of you, dear readers, who have ever struggled from the old cobbler's shoes syndrome, know and appreciate that it is often much trickier to deliver results for yourself than it is creating them for your clients.

The evolution of a brand

I am fascinated with the process of developing brands and that is exactly how Hartley & Soul came into being – it was not invented, it was developed – it evolved.

Marianne was – and is – a magnificent designer. This was exactly what she came to London to do – design. Temp, freelance, full time. This is usually how it goes. She worked with big clients on demanding accounts and it was fine for a bit, but it did not feel quite right. Perhaps it was the pace, perhaps it was the space, but something did not quite fit in.

Exploration

She decided to change it and created her first brand, the Jam Factory. It was a sweet business that allowed her to get more involved with the projects she created. It was a way of getting underneath the skin of the business and see what it really tastes like. However, that too turned out not to be enough. After a while, Marianne discovered that she somehow outgrew this format. She wanted something different. To figure out what that *something else* is, she analysed what makes her happy about the design.

Inner peace

As a child, Marianne wanted to be either a potter or a weaver. She also liked drawing very much – drawing nature, most of all. The trees, the sea – these are the elements that gave her balance – soothed and healed, in a manner of speaking. Hence came healing designs. Marianne believes that beauty can be healing. I am inclined to agree with her.

When we started talking about healing designs and possible applications of this philosophy, our interview morphed into a brainstorming session. We suddenly started discussing applications in urban design, cooperation with interior designers, its relationship with performance in the workplace, possible university courses on the subject, how the book could... would... will look like. When you think about your brand and you stumble across a thought, an idea that makes all those around you contribute and act in sync – hold on to it, this is the heart of it.

For Marianne, this is healing designs.

Designing from the inside

Healing designs are creations that make you feel better. We all know them when we see them – they are soothing, inspiring, reassuring. Marianne creates them and investigates the thinking behind them. She is very knowledgeable about Eastern and Western philosophies and combines them to help modern humans connect with beauty.

Her thinking about design and its role in modern life reminds me of creating mandalas for the contemporary minds. Works of art to serve a purpose, ones that are designed to bring us appreciation of what's around us and perhaps a little grain of peace.

For now, she is delivering that experience to her clients – creating beautiful designs and irresistible identities. To me, this is bigger than business design – it may start there, but I cannot believe it will be contained in that format for long. Time for another evolutionary step approaches.

I am very grateful to have been allowed a peek into what's inside, and I cannot wait to see what comes next.

WHY A BRAND HERO?

I admire Marianne's brand because she had the courage to allow herself to grow. She created Jam Factory because it was who she was then and it was an appropriate outlet for her creativity. However, she was sensitive to change and sensible enough to act when the time came to move on. She searched for what works within herself – with the help of a mentor – and grew her brand to represent her true self at this point in time. Brand is a living thing – it grows and develops with the people involved in it. Strong brands notice when the time comes to make the next step.

MY LESSONS FROM THIS CONVERSATION
1. Evolution is a necessary element of a strong brand
2. Only you can answer the question *"what is it that you really want to do?"*
3. You will only find the answer if you play to your strengths

ELEMENTS OF A STRONG BRAND
- HEART
- SOUL
- BEAUTY

INSPIRATION
Works of Dalai Lama

MOTTO
"It comes from within"

FIND OUT MORE
- Visit the website http://www.hartleyandsoul.com
- Find her on LinkedIn (look for Marianne Hartley)
- Discover them on Facebook facebook.com/HartleyandSoul
- Follow them on Twitter @HartleySoul
- ...and Pinterest pinterest.com/mariannehartley/

Wat is the source of your brand?

NATALIE HAVERSTOCK, MISS BALLOONIVERSE

Name of business: Miss Ballooniverse
Founder: Natalie Haverstock
Years in business: Since 2008
Speciality: Entertainment
Location: London
Reach: International
Key to success: Finding what fits your personality
Biggest challenge for businesses: Keeping on top of day-to-day activities and being ready for the increase of interest and the number of enquiries to deal with
Greatest asset: Attitude

HAPPINESS ON A STRING

First thing I noticed was a hat. It towered over a crowded room filled with entrepreneurs immersed in post-event conversations. It was intriguing and eye-catching; however, it was almost a year after that first encounter that we exchanged emails and finally met. We decided to arrange a London tête-à-tête. When arranging a date, there was an obstacle, however.

"My schedule is a bit tight. I will be teaching at the balloon convention in Las Vegas (don't laugh, these things actually exist)..."

After reading that sentence I knew it was going to be worth the wait. Yet, the anticipation was unbearable. When the day finally came, the heavens above London opened and it was gloomy, dark and uninviting. The conversation, however, was anything but.

Entertainment is a serious business

Natalie offstage is just the same bubbly personality you see making magic with balloons. The same gumption, openness and welcoming attitude. This approach makes you want to join in the fun, and her enthusiasm is contagious. She has the ability to make you feel at ease and at home. One glimpse of Natalie, and you can grasp what is the character of the brand. This permeates through her employees, website, videos... Each medium is an expression confirming and reinforcing brand values. Her team is her brand in action, from their attitude to their attire (petticoats for ladies and a dapper suit for the one gent in the team).

Ballooning

How do you start in ballooning? However unlikely that may sound, Natalie got headhunted. A friend of hers bought a balloon agency and after seeing Natalie on stage (she is an actor by background) wanted to grow a team; she joined and learned balloon art. And then, she got headhunted. When the recession hit, Natalie reverted to birthday parties; however, that led her to grow the brand organically. As they tend to, most birthday parties happened at the weekend, and so, as an idea to increase the business and boost its Monday to Friday activities, she wanted to grow role-play team-building events for corporates. Balloons were popular props and she thought that once she was good enough with them, she could put something together to utilise them as building blocks of corporate entertainment. So, she did.

It brightened up many an early morning networking event. It couldn't fail to when, among suits, you have a lady in a black polka dot dress with a red petticoat and a life-size balloon sculpture. The world of balloon art, I will have you know, has long since developed beyond swords and dachshunds and it is serious business.

Bring out the big kid in everyone

Natalie is a pleasure to be around. She is an artiste and has a vibrant, creative personality. However, the conversation is not lofty but practical and down to earth. She knows her strengths well, she works hard on making them even stronger and she knows how to play to them.

She understood she needed to stand out and she created her stage identity – Miss Ballooniverse – that radiates 1950s chic. It's vivacious and noticeable, reinforced by that great smile. I challenge you to find one photo of Miss Ballooniverse where she is out of character. She is the director, screenwriter and star of her brand. And, she is proficient. She would be a star at one of Elton John's parties, no doubt.

WHY A BRAND HERO?

Entrepreneur at heart

She started her first venture at the age of 18, when, with £1,000 of inheritance money, she created a photography and design studio and managed creative projects for small businesses. Then acting beckoned and, in truth, took over. However, the entrepreneurial bug remained. Perhaps this is one of the reasons that makes her aware that it all begins with the right approach. Skills can be taught, but in any business, especially in one that deals with clients face to face, attitude has to be right from the onset; you either have it, or you will be unhappy in this line of work. She is a glowing example of how to do it right.

So much so that she rarely needs to explain what she does – her work speaks for her. I suppose she's one of the pioneers in bringing balloon art out of the realm of children's birthday parties. She was inspired by magic and magicians: *"their websites are cool"*. She observed what they do right, put her own twist on it and developed the profile of Miss Ballooniverse.

She is very aware of what fits Miss Ballooniverse and what does not. You won't find twee. But you will find glamour, giggles, gumption and quality, in abundance.

"It's my dream job, I get paid to go to parties," she says.

She gives back a lot as well, working with Starlight Foundation and Rays of Sunshine. She believes in magic. And she carries it with her and pours it into her brand. Because of that, she is my brand hero.

MY LESSONS

1. Whether the name of the business contains your name or

not, you need to be your brand
2. Find a way to stand out, that brings what's the best in you
3. Respect your art

ELEMENTS OF A STRONG BRAND
- PERSONALITY
- CONFIDENCE
- BEING THE BEST FOR YOUR CLIENTS

MOTTO
It's not a credo per se, but two sentences that Natalie used during our conversation, that I believe fit this category: *"Clients are your brand ambassadors,"* and *"Remember to keep your sparkle going."*

FIND OUT MORE
- Visit their website missballooniverse.co.uk (do not miss their e-book the Amazing Adventures of Miss Ballooniverse)
- Follow them on Twitter
- Find them on Facebook/Miss-Ballooniverse
- Watch them on YouTube
- pin them on Pinterest
- There's Google+ as well
- ...and Flickr

Which elements of your personality are the most prominent within your brand?

HOLLY HELT, CHIKI TEA

Name of business: Chiki Tea
Founder: Holly Helt
Years in business: Since 2012
Speciality: Japanese green tea experience
Location: Nakatsu, Kyushu, Japan
Reach: International
Key to success: Appreciation of life and not compromising on quality
Greatest asset: Philosophy, as it created their product and developed the experience

Matcha, a fine green tea, is at the core of the business – this is a premium product, often costing as much as £20 per cup; Holly could not agree to that and searched for a superior matcha (which involved taste tests with three generations of tea ceremony masters) at an affordable price.

A CHIKI WAY OF LIFE

Get a little taste of Chiki

Holly Helt's posts on Facebook caught my eye some time ago – always colourful and full of enthusiasm. As we have never actually met, I hoped that she would agree to take part in this project, but I had no way of knowing. My fears were misplaced – she answered promptly and with fervour. We had a Skype chat and she began by giving me a tour of the tea shop, introducing me to her staff and waving to customers. She was open and hospitable throughout. You sometimes meet people, have a conversation, then don't see them for a while, but when you do meet again you pick up where you left it effortlessly. This is how I felt – included.

Home in every drop

When it comes to Chiki Tea I get this feeling of being welcome when I come across the brand via Facebook or Twitter, or in a direct conversation. I have never visited the company, but this is just a matter of time. I am already part of the experience. Such is the strength of this brand. And this happened so effortlessly – for me, the recipient. Holly and the team have worked very hard to make it easy for me, and to give their clients a place where they can so easily feel like they belong.

They did it by creating a space they belong to themselves.

Deep purple, green tea and chocolate

Holly grew up in Japan and basing Chiki Tea in Nakatsu is her way of repaying what she received from this culture. However, Chiki Tea is a British company. It's worth noting that Holly's spent most of her professional life in the corporate world. Holly worked in the City for years and travelled the world before she arrived at the merger of what Holly loves most in the East and West: the goodness of green tea and the sweetness of a triple choc brownie. There's no other place that combines the two this way! This is how she has always experienced it and now she shares it with her audience.

Something old, something new. It turns out this approach really appeals to the younger generation of Japan. Traditional tea ceremonies, although beautiful and majestic, became too rigid for the young spirits of this modern country. Chiki Tea offers all the benefits of quality tea without the boundaries of the convention. This strategy of going away from tradition actually brings the younger generation closer to its essence – the appreciation of the moment and the company.

Chiki Tea is bringing the young back to the culture through a modern doorway.

It also helps that you cannot find their signature matcha shots, smoothies and popsicles anywhere else. You could say these are *on trend*, but I think you would be wrong. This is not a brand that cares about the fashion. They created their own style. You see it in every element, from the packaging, through to the illustrations in the book, to (most importantly) the behaviour of the staff. This echoes through clients. Everyone is included.

For now, you have to visit Kyushu to fully immerse yourself in the Chiki Tea experience. For now, they are focusing on widening their reach in Japan. Then, if the time is right, they will perhaps come to England. When this happens, it will be a good day.

WHY A BRAND HERO?

Holly said one thing that resonates with me very strongly – she does not believe in competition. They have a lovely tea room as a neighbour. And that is just it, it is their neighbour. There is no fear, no anxiety about the 'what ifs'. There is awareness, appreciation, confidence and hard work – but it is a labour of love. It transpires. That is why Holly Helt and Chiki Tea are my brand heroes.

MY LESSON FROM THIS CONVERSATION

1. Love life
2. Be true to yourself
3. When you have the above, you are creating a culture around your brand

ELEMENTS OF A STRONG BRAND

- AUTHENTICITY
- SPIRIT
- CULTURE

INSPIRATION

Starbucks – on leadership, development and business growth

MOTTO

"Life is short. Enjoy it."

DISCOVER MORE

- Visit their website chikitea.com
- Follow them on Twitter @ChikiTea
- Find them on Facebook @ChikiTeaTime

Holly Helt's personal story is amazing. I am really grateful that she shared this with me and I am sure another book could be written about it. She speaks with such kindness and grace about various elements of life that led her to this moment, and this softness makes her a very strong personal brand as well. If you ever come across an event with her as a speaker, go.

Who is your greatest competitor? What if they could become your brand's partner?

AARON JONES, FIKAY FASHION

Name of business: Fikay Fashion
Founder: Aaron Jones
Years in business: Since 2012
Speciality: Ethically Producing High Quality Goods That Inspire Change
Location: London
Reach: International
Key to success: Concentration, motivation and cash flow
Biggest challenge for businesses: Prioritisation and task completion; and cash flow
Greatest asset: Network

ETHICAL REALITY

I first heard about Aaron when he was a student at the Essex Business School; he was introduced to me as this amazing young guy who has this incredible story and does cool things with fashion. I thought OK, great, sounds wonderful. Slightly improbable, but delightful nonetheless. Little did I know that the truth was even more impressive. Only in his early twenties and he is on a mission to make our reality an ethical one, with decent chances for everyone who wants to make use of the opportunities.

Since then Aaron moved from Southend-on-Sea to London and is growing Fikay from one concept to becoming an umbrella brand for ethical fashion initiatives. We meet over pizza to talk Fikay brand and the reality of life in fashion.

... and they heard: *"Fiiikaaaayyy!"*

Students on a gap year travelling around Cambodia. The two explorers are fascinated by the beauty of the country and petrified by the poverty woven into the landscape. The discrepancy is huge. One evening they were deliberating the seriousness of the issue, when a boy dive-bombed into a pool with a joyful shout "Fiiikaaay!" In their minds, that was the epitome of what life should be; that word encompassed the naiveté, hope and joy. That is where the name of the brand comes from.

First steps

The beginnings were… spartan, shall we say. Now they have professional storage, but there were times when Aaron and the stock shared the same room. These are the charms of launching a venture when you are a student. Aaron has always been the leader of this project; however, he was smart enough to look around for help. From tutors to colleagues, he looked for expertise hidden within his network and he used his talent to grow his circle of influence. Business mentorship, funding, graphic design, brand development strategy – he was able to partner with and collaborate with individuals and organisations that could support him. I commend him for that; no doubt this approach is why he managed to lift the project off the ground. Of course, organising this support network and making sure he had products and suppliers lined up took a vast amount of time, dedication and engagement. How he was able to complete his degree at the same time, I shall never know.

The tale of how Fikay came into being is a romantic one, and to this day Aaron remains a romantic; that is how I see him. He is still motivated by that Fikay spirit and he's adamant it is visible in every product they design, on every label, through all of their channels. The labels tell the story of the maker, so you are really connected with the change you, as a client, are contributing to making.

The connection

Fikay builds bridges between manufacturers in the Far East and decent living conditions, as well as designers closer to home and their market.

They are promoting an ethical approach to fashion, but they are not angry with their movement. They are doing their best to make the right change. They give us the opportunity to support them and they are very straightforward about it. One of my favourite quotes from Aaron is *"Fikay is all about successful living without screwing everyone over."*

And they are open about it. The language is straightforward and practical. The idea is quite romantic, but the expression is well grounded. The hand, their logo, represents the acts of openness and kindness and I see it as an act of volunteering to join and saying *"that's enough"* to all that is wrong and can be improved.

Recognition

Fikay is growing and has already been recognised by many as the one to watch by being awarded the Ernst & Young Future 50 Award, the Intuit Top 100, the Virgin Media Pioneers Award... to name but a few. The brand now continues to grow its presence online.

Next steps

However, Aaron and his team are not resting on their laurels. There is too much to be done, at both ends of the world. Closer to home, they are managing the SEE Fashion project, which gives young designers an opportunity to prove their concept and find a route to market. Aaron and the Fikay spirit are doing well.

WHY A BRAND HERO?

What's impressive about this brand is that they are changing the world – their suppliers can afford to send their children to school, their designers get access to the market, mentors and funding as well. What is, to me, amazing, is that this ethical context, although at the core of Fikay's activities, is almost an element of added value to the client. We do not have to choose between design and ethics, they are giving us a stunning tool to improve the reality we live in and feel good about it. Fikay and the team give me faith that there is always someone in this world doing good. They do it really well. For that, they are my brand heroes.

MY LESSONS FROM THIS CONVERSATION

1. Find your Fikay. It will drive you forward, keep you on track and help you work through the more challenging moments
2. Don't go it alone – there is expertise in your network;

having the courage to ask, for it pays off
3. Look ahead and mind the cash flow

ELEMENTS OF A STRONG BRAND
- SPIRIT
- HONESTY
- RELIABILITY

MOTTO
"If God created the world in six days, then the Devil invented multitasking on the seventh."

FIND OUT MORE
- Visit fikay.co.uk
- Find them on LinkedIn (look for Aaron Jones)
- Look them up on Facebook at facebook.com/FikayEcoFashion
- Follow them on Twitter at twitter.com/fikayfashion

What is the spirit of your brand?

JIM JORDAN, JIM JORDAN CONSULTANCY

Name of business: Jim Jordan Consultancy
Founder: Jim Jordan
Years in business: Since 2005
Speciality: Making businesses profitable
Location: London and South East
Reach: National
Key to success: Untamed ambition and realistic goals
Biggest challenge for businesses: Focus
Greatest asset: Network

USE WHAT YOU HAVE TO GET WHAT YOU NEED

I met Jim Jordan ages ago at a networking meeting. For two years, we have been meeting weekly, and we have observed each other's pitching and presentation skills. We saw each other's businesses evolve. In the meantime, we became friends. We sometimes even consulted with each other's clients and so I was able to observe Jim Jordan Consultancy in front of a client and witness the 'behind the scenes'. I am pleased to say that he is himself on both sides of the curtain. He is true to his brand and that helps him reveal the true nature of his clients' brands. So, what is his brand?

Results-orientated, confident, not overwhelming. Calm, not intimidating. Decisive, not bullying.

Jim has impressive experience. To give you a glimpse, it includes hundreds of hours of training delivered by some of the most well-known names in the coaching world: Tony Robbins and Richard

Bandler and Peter Thomson. Also, achievements such as being the youngest manager promoted into Oxford Street for Clarks Shoes in the 80s and delivering strategies that enabled a team to turn the store around from making a loss to making a profit… and one with six zeros, too. And consistently being Top Performing Regional Manager for an impressive 11 years. He also talks proudly about his time as Head of Retail in Ireland in the 90s where he turned a 10-year loss-making region into making substantial profits within two years.

All for one, one for all

His success was built on the ability to observe and notice people's strengths. Then designing systems that allowed team members to exhibit their talents: making it possible for them to shine as individuals and benefit from the strengths of a team.

Having stepped out of the corporate world, he implements his knowledge and know-how empowering British and Irish small and medium businesses. Including himself – re-engineering himself as a solopreneur and building a career from scratch was a challenge. One that proved hard, but useful, as it brought Jim closer to his clients. Jim is someone you can trust because he is genuinely on your side.

The shift of power

He could, easily, use all his experience and list his certificates to intimidate prospective clients and business partners into obedient silence. Instead, he uses it to give them confidence. He is not exactly hiding all his achievements, but whenever he speaks about them, he does it very matter-of-factly. And it works. Say you meet for the first time: you just have a pleasant conversation with a friendly, reasonable and knowledgeable guy. It is only after the conversation that you realise you mostly talked about yourself and, somehow, between the lines, solved one or two marketing and leadership issues you have been having. Then you go to chat with Jim again and you find more clarity. He never offers a one-fits-all solution, but finds shrewd suggestions for you to implement – for you are the one who know your business best; and in conversation you gain his perspective, and this viewpoint can be immensely useful. Then you find there is no time to be intimidated, you are friends already.

Use what you have, and you have more than you see

I admire Jim for his knowledge and experience, but even more for the fact that he admitted he spent too much time shying away from the digital platforms. As a professional in the coaching industry, he knew the potential of this platform and he had to overcome his own perceptions of himself to be able to stand in front of camera, to record that first interview, to write a book and publish it. Because I know him personally, I am grateful to him for that – it makes him human :) and it also shows that other humans, of which I am one, can overcome their own perceptions of themselves as well.

Good strategy, but it is most effective within a 1-2-1 setting. Due to its intimate nature, that type of work has its limitations – you are working with only one person at a time. It is great if you are matched with a client that can truly benefit from your knowledge, but it can be a very time-expensive route to market. Coming from a corporate background, Jim knew that and used his experience to scale up his operations.

That is why you can find Jim more and more as a speaker at conferences, leading webinars and courses. Whichever platform he uses – and I am pleased to see him and his IP digitalised more every year – he uses the same strategy: allowing businesses – brands – to gain perspective and learn something useful during each interaction. I have known him since 2010 and no conversation was left without some sort of insight helping. That is a skill. And this is also something I believe makes a good brand: acting so that each contact, touchpoint, interaction, benefits those around you, clients or not.

Jim shows his clients they can achieve that, too.

WHY A BRAND HERO?

Jim never withholds good advice when he is asked for it. He nudges business people on to the right path in a very subtle way, by asking simple, small questions that often have a big effect. He understands how important it is for business founders, for people, to realise these things themselves. That is what makes strategies stick, that is how we make them our own. It makes us more likely to succeed.

This is why Jim Jordan is my brand hero.

MY LESSONS

1. Ambition can be overwhelming, attainable goals make it achievable
2. Being realistic about what you currently have will help you grow
3. We often underplay how good we are and how much we have achieved in order not to intimidate our clients, friends… which is actually a disservice to them: being truthful about your own achievements is empowering (but I

found it also can be surprisingly hard!)

ELEMENTS OF A STRONG BRAND
- PURPOSE
- HUMAN ASPECT
- PERSPECTIVE

MOTTO
"Focus on the 20% of activities that will give you 80% of your results", and
*"It's people with a purpose that make profits. All they need is confidence in
themselves as well as a well-executed strategy."*

Find out more a
- Visit his website: jimjordanconsultancy.com
or www.businessgrowth-success.com
or smallbusinessmarketing-success.com
- Find him on LinkedIn: linkedin.com/in/Jim Jordan
- Follow him on Facebook: Jim Jordan
- Add his book to your Kindle collection: *10 Secrets of Business
  Growth Success: Out Sell, Out Market and Out Think Your
  Competition*

*What resource do
you already have
to get what you
need?*

HEATHER KATSONGA WOODWARD, NENO NATURAL

Name of business: Neno Natural
Founder: Heather Katsonga Woodward
Years in business: Since 2013
Speciality: Natural haircare products
Location: London
Reach: International
Key to success: Know your audience
Biggest challenge for businesses: Finding the right people to work with on product development
Greatest asset: IP

YOU DON'T BECOME A BILLIONAIRE BY BEING AVERAGE

She has infectious enthusiasm and a big smile. She speaks fast and smiles a lot. There is a reason for that – she knows it all. I mean ALL of what there is to know about her business. And, if anything new crops up, she's on it in seconds. She is one fearsome businesswoman with an international reach.

"I did not have to guess what their problems were. They told me."
~ Heather Katsonga Woodward

At the time of going to print, in May 2017, Natural Hair Growth by Neno Natural YouTube channel has 19,000 subscribers and Facebook over 400,000.

It started with a blog about hair issues and possible solutions. When it got 5,000 followers within the first month, Heather knew she was on to something good.

They posted questions, she answered – this proved to be a winning formula. This relationship lies at the core of her business, which now incorporates Neno Natural haircare products (hair oils and a new product line dedicated to dry hair, available later this year), hair accessories, DIY hair product development book series, and a business development programme *How to Build a 6-figure Product Business*. Every element of this empire revolves – and evolves – around this core ability: listening to customers.

Heather created a brand that makes its mark on a very competitive market. On one end of the scale, we have mass-produced products that are created with the most common denominator in mind; they sell on volume. On the other end, we have boutique shops with hand-made beauty products, often produced in low quantities, with a very short shelf life. Neno Natural sits in between the two, bringing quality ingredients and personalised packages to wider audiences.

"People want better quality, a better experience. And I offer all these lovely natural ingredients that people want."
~ Heather Katsonga Woodward

And Heather offers them that. When buying elsewhere, you have to choose individual pots and bottles that don't necessarily give you the best results. Neno gives you a set. Simple. Sorted.

"People want advice and guidance." ~ Heather Katsonga Woodward

Supermarkets tend to sell large volumes fast. Neno focuses on what is really needed. It works – read comments on her website; it is a voice of a true and loyal following.

What started with a blog, evolved into a business that does well in America and now comes to the UK. What's next? Partnership with a company that will help distribute the products internationally, especially across Africa. *"If we could get that,"* says Heather, *"the world would be our oyster."*

WHY A BRAND HERO?

She is unstoppable. Her enthusiasm is infectious and she knows what she wants to do. Then she does it.

Heather believes in doing things right. *"No product will work for everyone, but every product will work for someone,"* she says.

"I want to be recognised by a good, small niche of people that will love the brand. I think it's better to have 10,000 people that love Neno Natural than a million that just kinda like it."

Neno Natural truly serves their customers. They know them well. They even create events for them, keeping the relationship real and engagement authentic. This seems to be the key to making sure their answers to clients' problems stay relevant and their products sought after.

ELEMENTS OF A STRONG BRAND
- KNOWLEDGEABLE
- QUALITY CONTENDER
- GO-GETTER

INSPIRATION
- Richard Branson
- Oprah Winfrey
- Sara Blakely
- Kim Love – Founder of Luv Naturals, another haircare brand

MOTTO
"Shoot for the moon. Even if you miss, you'll still be among the stars."

FIND OUT MORE
- Visit her website nenonatural.com
- YouTube channel Natural Hair Growth by Neno Natural
- Find them on Facebook /LongHealthyHair
- ...and Twitter @NenoNatural

What are your clients telling you?

DANIEL KENNING, SPLENDID ENGINEERING & GATE

Name of business: Splendid Engineering & Global Association for Transitional Engineering (GATE)
Founder: Daniel Kenning (GATE co-founder)
Years in business: Since 2001
Speciality: Transition engineering
Location: Essex
Reach: International
Key to success: Education, networking, collaboration
Greatest asset: Having been taught how to think differently

WE CAN DO THIS THING THAT IS GOOD FOR THE WORLD OF TODAY AND TOMORROW

He is on a quest of changing the way the world thinks about sustainability and its practices. He begins with business management, but wants his idea to change nations. Can he do it? The Impressive words behind his name[1] and the fact that he is cooperating with Susan Krumdieck, Professor in Mechanical Engineering at Canterbury University in New Zealand, says *yes*.

Today he patiently develops assets to make a real change. Revolutions may be impressive, but he wants to initiate a gentler process – start

---

1   Those impressive words are: Chartered Mechanical Engineer and Energy Engineer, and Chartered Environmentalist, Fellow of the Institution of Mechanical Engineers, a member of the Energy Institute and an Associate of the Institution of Environmental Management and Assessment. *"They are there as signposts to potential clients, and may seem pompous out of context. They tell clients "I'm a qualified and experienced engineer whose contribution to the profession is recognised by my peers. So I'm good to employ,"* says Daniel.

from where you are and improve the world, step by step.

Sustainability – a *nice to have* but a sine qua non for the survival of humanity

Imagine you need to go through a small doorway. You don't bend by 1% this year and 3% next year. If you really want to get through, you will adjust your position to fit the frame and go to the other side. Otherwise you get stuck.

That, in a nutshell, is what transition engineering is about. Changing what's un-sustainable into a format that allows the change to happen. It involves logistics, systems, management – across the board. This transformation includes all industries – not only automotive, not only oil and gas. It may well start with them, and their adjustments may be more visible than changes small offices make, but it includes us all. It is about systems that we as businesses, and ultimately as individuals, depend on.

Going through the GATE

You have to realise one thing – sustainability is not synonymous with being vegetarian and drinking fair trade coffee. Managing resources is not a green policy, its logic. *"If you look at the whole history of engineering since the industrial revolution, every generation of engineers has delivered more; but they have had more and more resources to use, and in the future our challenge is going to be delivering enough rather than just always more and more – with less resources,"* says Daniel. Transition engineering is a strategy to help business adapt to the new order, which is inevitably coming.

By the way, he found her when he first used the phrase 'transition engineering' and, according to Google, she was the only other person using this term. He approached her and now they are collaborating on a project, supporting each other's efforts to educate and increase the profile of their brands.

This change has begun, but the process is slow. That is why Daniel is cooperating with Professor Krumdieck, with whom he's co-creating GATE – Global Association for Transition Engineering.

GATE is going to be a charity, driving the change, bringing it to our, the public's, attention. I think it's a fitting strategy to grow the brand whose product is relevant to all. Still, they were able to find their niche and are working their way up from there. It's another example of how being focused helps you make more impact and eventually increases your reach.

Hopefully, it will lead to fulfilling their business ambitions – advising the UK government on transition engineering. *"These days engineers are a bit too timid, I think,"* admits Daniel. *"We need to get back to that level where the policymakers phone us up to ask us what they should do."*

WHY A BRAND HERO?
Protesting against a chemical factory is not part of the plan

Although he mentions Isambard Kingdom Brunel[2] and Michael Braungart[3] as engineering icons, he believes protesting is not the right way to make lasting developments. He wants to begin a dialogue that will lead to sustainable change.

However, I think he will need some of Brunel's and Braungart's imagination-grabbing power to help this cause. And Edward de Bono's[4] ability to teach lateral thinking as a skill. Having said that, for the quest that he dedicated his career to, he is my brand hero.

MY LESSONS FROM THIS CONVERSATION
1. Speaking plainly, no matter how technical the 'behind the scenes' language is
2. Seek partnerships, even from the other side of the world
3. Aim high

ELEMENTS OF A STRONG BRAND
- IMAGINATION-GRABBING VISION
- SPEAKING PLAINLY, NO MATTER HOW TECHNICAL THE 'BEHIND THE SCENES' LANGUAGE IS
- STAYING RELEVANT

2   Isambard Kingdom Brunel marched to Westminster to stand in the Houses of Parliament, to influence the change of the law, enabling him to build the railway from London to Bristol.

3   When Michael Braungart was a young man, in his twenties, he climbed to the top of the chimney at the BASF chemical factory to force them to switch off the factory – it was on Christmas Eve in Cologne, Germany. He managed to have a private conversation with the Chief Executive, who climbed the chimney as well, and he promised to shut down the company, even if Michael Braungart wasn't at the top of the chimney.

4   Edward de Bono is credited with inventing the concept of Lateral Thinking and being the world leader for teaching of thinking as a skill.

INSPIRATION

- Michael Braungart
- Jonathon Porritt
- Richard Branson
- Edward de Bono

MOTTO

"You can win much better by campaigning for something than campaigning against something" ...also *"Towards better"* and *"Vision and transition – helping you to see the future and achieve it"*

FIND OUT MORE

- visit splendidengineering.co.uk

What is your vision?

HASEENA LATHEEF, DFYNORM

Name of business: DFYNorm (Defy the Norm)
Founder: Haseena Latheef
Years in business: Since 2014
Speciality: Fashion, public speaking, personal development
Location: London
Reach: International
Key to success: Celebrating humanity and being the change you wish to see in the world
Biggest challenge for businesses: Conscientious marketing, caring about the impact on people and environment
Greatest asset: Spirit and courage to defy the norms

FASHION CONSCIOUS

Haseena is loquacious but chooses her words wisely. Her thoughts are composed and yet the tale is candid. We meet at the food court in the City. The service is bad, but the fact that no one cares about us at the table gives us the space we need to talk. This is the description of the impression Haseena and DFYNorm made on me that day.

There is nothing more powerful than an idea whose time has come

To sketch the context, I need to tell you a little bit about the upbringing of the brand's creator.

Beauty or *beautiful* is what her name means. She did not feel the beauty her name described. It took time for Haseena to appreciate that what sets individuals apart, what makes them stand out – although it may at times feel like a burden – should be celebrated.

Her hobby was, for a time, creating dresses for paper dolls. However,

DFYNorm own the whole supply chain and process, from conception to completion. This is very different from most fashion companies and makes them practically a design house with their own production facility. It makes them stand out from most brands, not only start-up brands. It helps DFYNorm maintain quality control and keep an eye on ethical standards.

fashion wasn't considered a serious career for a studious student. Being a doctor or an engineer was supposed to be her future.

Raised in Dubai, in a conservative family, and having attended an American school, she grew up into two societal models; however, having met Haseena and observing her since, it seems to me that her spirit was not the one to conform.

Destiny

Due to a clerical error, her architecture school application got filed as one for a business school. Business was supposed to be her second choice and by the time she found out it was too late. This was an American university. Even though the subjects weren't challenging enough, I'd hazard a guess that the cultural exposure stirred something in her spirit. She observed, studied and learned, and maths was supplemented by literature and philosophy. Her view grew and I suppose it outgrew the bounds of the society in which she existed.

"I think reading a lot and being curious about the world out there also helped shape a broader perspective (beyond just attending university)"
~ Haseena Latheef

Life brought her to London in 2013 and today she's developing this brand that is an amazing concept. This is fashion that defies conforming to fashion in order to feel beautiful – the status quo of the public. Rather she focuses on and emphasises the beauty that exists.

She does it through sourcing ethical materials, choosing her partnerships very carefully to support the premise of empowerment and ethics and the thing that captured my mind completely: promoting role models. Haseena chooses real-life heroes – accomplished businesswomen, authors and mentors – to style her clothing lines.

(R)evolution

It is a brilliant and (sadly) a revolutionary concept. Her catwalk, her lookbook, shows us people to look up to – people with knowledge, experience and kind spirit.

I can't wait for the fashion world to start copying her! She shows us, the public, that beauty already exists and needs only to be enhanced, rather than superimposed. We should not aspire to fit the size, but wear our own shapes with pride and find what complements them.

Role models

She creates the tools with which her clients can highlight their own beauty. It's elegant, caring and so very human. It is about changing the norms, but the language DFYNorm use and the atmosphere they create is kind. Even their logo is a bit unruly with its typeface; yet it is easy to read, there are no obstacles there, and the brand with its presence makes the first step towards the audience.

What I really like is that DFYNorm uses the channels we are used to (website, Facebook, Twitter) to share thrilling ideas. Usual mediums are utilised to convey uncommon thoughts. And, though the ideas are stirring, there is nothing militant or vindictive about DFYNorm. This is a revolution, though, do not get me wrong, as once you notice them and experience their story, you cannot un-notice it. Not that you would want to.

WHY A BRAND HERO?

DFYNorm's strapline is *"wear your heart"* and they do it themselves. It's a fashion with mind, heart and soul. Each garment is more than meets the eye.

Its source: the idea behind the design, the whole story. And the movement of using role models to showcase fashion lines is inspired.

Haseena defies norms that need improving and that is why she and her brand are my heroes.

LESSONS FROM THIS CONVERSATION

1. Inspiring clients to do better helps you create a following
2. Embodying the spirit of your brand should be a given
3. Being human is a necessity 4. Not giving up is hard, but worth it
4. Surrounding yourself with people you look up to is one of the best things you can do

ELEMENTS OF A STRONG BRAND
- BEAUTY OF THE HEART
- SUBSTANCE THAT SUPPORTS AMBITIOUS SPIRIT
- CONSTANT INSPIRATION TO BE BETTER

MOTTO
"Pursue your authenticity"

DISCOVER MORE
- Visit their website https://www.dfynorm.com/
- Find them on facebook.com/dfynorm
- Follow them on @DFYnorm

How does your brand inspire your clients?

ANGELA MAKEPEACE, MOTION GRAPHICS STUDIO

Name of business: Motion Graphics Studio
Founder: Angela Makepeace
Years in business: Since 2012
Speciality: Explainer videos
Location: Colchester, Essex
Reach: UK & USA
Key to success: Play to your strengths
Greatest asset: How much we love what we do

FOLLOW YOUR GUT

If you were to imagine a person who is very content with where they are and what they are doing, getting optimistically excited by every new assignment and always (always!) smiling when talking about their work, you would be thinking of Angela Makepeace. We spoke over the phone and I could hear her smiling. When I think about this conversation, one word comes to mind: bright.

The animated one

You probably heard this type of story before. You work for someone, get experience, learn a thing or two. Then you notice the limitations of your position. The fact is that in some cases you work for your manager more than you do for the actual client. Once you notice that the spectrum of the decision-making process in which you are involved is smaller than you had hoped for, you cannot un-notice it. Some are comfortable with that safety net of filters diluting responsibility. Others choose a different way. Angela did just that.

Only hers was a better way.

This is why...

1. She trusts herself

The business may be relatively young, but Angela is not a newbie in the industry. She's spent years working as an animator, developing videos for agencies, learning from her bosses. That, of course, gave her experience in the day-to-day of animation, but also taught her how to recognise trends, and deal (or not deal) with clients, managing departments, expectations. That understanding is crucial to developing her brand. It strengthens her core abilities and means that she can build a better business.

2. She does not get distracted

"It scares me to death that I would ever have to get back to a 'proper' job." ~ Angela Makepeace

For making videos, according to Angela, is not a proper job – she enjoys it too much. So she does everything to keep it that way. Luckily for her, she never had a problem with self-discipline. Even working from home, there was never a problem with daytime TV. When she is at work, she works. At the same time she enjoys the freedom and the balance of the on-off time. I have to admit, I envy her that (note to self – focus: balance).

3. She gets excited about every single project

Even when she speaks about what is in the pipeline she lights up. That is not naivety, she is far too experienced for that. It is a sign of someone who's in the right place: they have the knowledge and are not afraid to share it (via blogs and instructive videos), and the experience to enjoy developing new scripts with confidence. That is joy. This enthusiasm is infectious... no wonder her clients are happy (see point no. 5).

4. She never stops learning

Listening to experiences of others is *a bottomless pit of information* on managing finances, contracts, branding and social media. This ability allows her to keep on top of things and generate fresh ideas, which is handy, as video is the future of communication. The lesson here is: stick to what you know but do not get stuck, keep adding on.

5. She's never going to be churning scripts

Angela has a clear definition of her business. Her studio produces short films, but it is not a factory and is not going to become one, if she can help it. Each client receives the full attention of her team. And it is going to stay that way – even if her studio evolves into the next Pixar. It is a nurturing relationship and both sides enjoy it. *"Having happy clients is a great experience,"* she says. *"But nothing was spoon-fed to us. Finding our own clients is one of our biggest successes. It's even better when they find us."*

And these are the reasons why she is my brand hero.

ELEMENTS OF A STRONG BRAND
- CONSISTENCY
- WARMTH
- MAKING CLIENTS HAPPY BY KEEPING YOUR TEAM HAPPY

INSPIRATION
Everything about Virgin; for keeping their staff happy, which boosts customer service, and for the way they develop their brand, the atmosphere they create around themselves, whether it's a finance product or a space travel venture.

MOTTO
"You are your choices, you can do what you feel is right"

FIND OUT MORE
- Visit her website angelamakepeace.co.uk
- Follow her on Twitter @angelamakepeace
- Find her on YouTube: angelamakepeace

What does your gut tell you about the direction of your brand?

JANE MALYON, THE ENGLISH CREAM TEA CO.

Name of business: The English Cream Tea Company
Founder: Jane Malyon
Years in business: Since 2012
Speciality: The cream tea experience, delivered via hampers, speciality jams and teas, and workshops
Location: Dunmow
Reach: International
Key to success: Passion and having the systems in place before you need them, allowing them to grow with the company and streamlining the development (*"When you grow, if one part is missing, it [the business] crumbles,"* comments Jane)
Biggest challenge for businesses: Distribution, developing relationships with buyers
Greatest asset: Husband and the team (*"No one person can do it all,"* concludes Jane Malyon)
Greatest achievement, so far: Breaking the Guinness World Record of most people having cream tea at the same time; this event was chosen over BBC appearances and TEDx talk, as it was *a masterclass in organisation*

FOR THE LOVE OF TEA, SCONES AND THE PEOPLE

Jane always loved the way afternoon tea brought the family together. She admired the ceremonial, the proper way of things. One afternoon she met an old lady who shared her love for fresh tea, cucumber sandwiches and smoked salmon. They talked about the extraordinary experience at the Savoy, to which the old lady said *"That was probably my last afternoon tea ever"*. Jane thought – that must not happen, there has to be a way to bring the afternoon tea to you. There wasn't, so she created one.

Two weeks later the outline of the English Cream Tea Co. was ready.

We meet at Jane's house and HQ of the business. The reception room is actually more of a showroom, but it's not your usual one. It's homely and it makes you want to sit straight and use nice phrases in a conversation, just because you are able to and because it's a pleasure.

Banter in a hamper, seriously

Cream tea is a very British thing. Every culture has its equivalent. An afternoon ritual bringing all family members together. It has its rules – the etiquette. But the protocol only enhances good manners: restraint, politeness, kindness (you need to think about the other person first), consideration (do acknowledge the company, notice them and appreciate the time spent together). Call me old-fashioned, but I find it quite liberating to know the rules and the order of proceedings in business and in life, actually. It allows me to find my space and feel more comfortable in a given situation. I suppose cream tea is a vehicle to teach this lesson. It is done with a smile and not a ruler hovering over your wrist. First of all, this cream tea comes to you. Secondly, it comes with instructions to help you fully enjoy the experience. They have got rid of the harsh and twee, leaving the *lovely* and the *tickety boo* of the affair.

Exporting quality time

On a more serious note, these are scones on a mission – to save the world, no less. *"You cannot hate someone you have shared a scone with,"* explains Jane. Most deals are struck over dinner – even Robert Cialdini[1] has written about that, so sharing a scone truly may be the first step to peace between nations… especially as these ones are made with butter, not margarine, and they fall apart in your fingers.

I do not suspect the fact that this business growth is driven by demand will come as a surprise to anyone. However, what you'll find

1   Robert Cialdini is a psychologist, author, speaker, and currently Regents' Professor Emeritus of Psychology and Marketing at Arizona State University. He is most known for his theory of influence described in his perhaps most famous book *Influence: The Psychology of Persuasion.*

baffling is that the biggest interest originates outside of the UK: Canada, the Americas and the Middle East request cream tea. For now, they can only have the jam and tea, but the team is working hard to make the *"very perishable"* scones and clotted cream available as well. That's the next task for those lovingly described by the brand creator as *scone gnomes*.

The fact that they are all truly engaged in the brand is clear when you meet the team and when you come across the fruits of their labour. The passion of the creators makes it a great brand to work with. They want to make it a worthwhile experience as their marketing team have shares in the business. That is brave, but it's a great way of ensuring that your team is truly 'putting the good' of the brand first.

WHY A BRAND HERO?

When you have a strong idea, the branding is a natural consequence of your mission. The English Cream Tea Co. is an exemplary example of how branding can be present in every molecule of the business – the packaging, the language, the experience, the taste. All comes from the idea Jane had four years ago and it is still true to it. That is its strength. You may have read about cream teas, tasted one with jam and cream, but after experiencing The English Cream Tea, you will know it is the only way. You will want to have it the only way. David Ogilvy said that branding is a way of claiming space in your client's mind. They have done it, and in a very tasteful way, too.

…Just have a taste of their scones, you will know what I'm talking about.

MY LESSONS FROM THIS CONVERSATION

1. Develop relationships and partnerships, they will stimulate and support your development
2. When you have a great idea, the branding flows through it
3. Find a mentor, find a mentor and find a mentor

ELEMENTS OF A STRONG BRAND

- SPIRIT, PRESENT IN EVERY COMMUNICATION
- RELEVANCY, BOTH TO YOUR VALUES AND YOUR AUDIENCE'S NEEDS
- TASTE

INSPIRATION
OR *"WHAT WOULD JESSICA FLETCHER DO?"*

How's that for a personal brand as an icon! I can see Jane and Jessica as kindred spirits though: both enjoy the finer things in life, they don't give in when faced with adversity, both are witty and resourceful, savoir vivre is an important ingredient of their recipe for a good life, and they love people and are spirited. And both are wonderful aunties.

MOTTO

"Enjoy the journey; it will keep you away from the regret."

P.S. On departure, she presents me with a tin of her grandfather's tea. In all the excitement, I left it on the table. What a shame, I will have to go back for it. I hope there will be scones…

HUNGRY FOR MORE?
- Visit their Facebook page @EnglishCreamTea
- Follow them on Twitter @EnglishCreamTea
- Visit their website englishcreamtea.com

How tasteful is the experience of your brand?

EDITH MILLER & CAROLINE TAPLIN, IDEAS HUB

Name of business: Ideas Hub Community Interest Organisation
Founder: Leonie Ramondt
Years in business: Since 2012
Speciality: Supporting community, business ideas and creative ventures from all walks of life
Location: Chelmsford
Reach: Local
Key to success: Focus on who you are now and what you want to achieve
Greatest asset: Volunteers and location (a lovely view of the park over the River Chelmer)

BUSINESS MIND, CREATIVE HEART

The context

They've just opened a few minutes ago but the place is full of activity. At the table in the back of the room, a business advisor is talking to an aspiring entrepreneur about her business plan. I am eavesdropping. They are talking about projections and the real cost of an event. Unexpected fees can really kill the cash flow, especially in the early stages, when businesses are working hard to gain momentum. The role of this place is to facilitate growth by providing space to work and guidance on how to make it more productive. After hours, this venue welcomes artists, poets, *Magic: The Gathering* players. It is a very funky space. This is Ideas Hub, Chelmsford. To find out about this initiative I talk to Caroline Taplin, programme coordinator, in person, and with Edith Miller, Hub Manager, via email.

The hub

I heard about this place a while ago but last week was my first visit. Let me tell you, if you are a start-up looking for a meeting space, or just a desk and a Wi-Fi to help you get your content out there, get yourself to the Ideas Hub. It is a shame spaces like this in Essex are few and far between. Funky décor (even in the loo!), fast Internet (… even in the loo…), coffee and access to support if you need it, is exactly what microbusinesses need to move them up the scale of development.

The people

They are working hard to make this place known and I hope this article will help them spread the word as I am really rooting for this venture.

The organisation is a charity, *"but it feels like taking a new business off the ground, which demands giant amounts of energy, efforts and hard work,"* says Edith Miller. I believe their biggest strength is the team. All volunteers; they decorated the place and they are the ingredient that brings it to life: open, welcoming, supportive.

The ideas

I can see a need for this kind of space. I used to use it myself as an office-on-the-go or a meeting space. Their vision reaches beyond obvious practical applications for the hub.

"Colchester fashioned itself as a creative city and London is a business centre. We see Chelmsford as a hub for creative businesses," says Caroline Taplin, Programme Coordinator. They help businesses from all walks of life. Whether you are a start-up looking for advice on your business plan or a medium-sized business that hit a rough patch and needs support in reigniting their vision or strategy, this is a place you should turn to. The past is the past; they look at where you are and who you are today, and help you figure out a better tomorrow. Be prepared for honest assessment, though, as they sport advice that helps make real change.

They go beyond business support. They seem to have become the place for diversity: 41 different nationalities so far and a much liked space for families. Also, they are growing in stature, with both councils involving us in their projects, such as a long-term art and culture strategy for Chelmsford, as well as working in cooperation on Ideas Hub's own initiatives.

If you are prepared to achieve something good, go to 1–4 Market Square, High Chelmer.

WHY A BRAND HERO?

It is a good idea to manage a charity like a business and it pays off – Ideas Hub is a very good example: since opening in 2012, they have tripled the income of the café, which is now offering a proper menu, and all still ethical and sustainable.

They are who they want to help. They want to support creative business and they are a creative space that is funding itself. They want to do it in an ethical way (their café sells ethically sourced snacks). They have a big vision of reinventing this corner of Chelmsford into a Soho space with Google vibe. They want to build a culture. I believe they are doing so already.

MY LESSONS
1. Having a product and a logo is not enough, the next challenge for them is get their name out there
2. Aim at creating a culture that is great for your brand
3. Choose your team wisely: working together they will become best ambassadors for your brand, divided they will turn into a capricious committee

ELEMENTS OF A STRONG BRAND
- CULTURE
- PEOPLE BELIEVING IN ONE GOAL
- TRUTH

INSPIRATION
Study Google as a business. The vibe, the culture, the service.

MOTTO
They did not express any one single motto, but when I now think about my day at the hub, I just think: *"It can be done."*

FIND OUT MORE
- Visit their website ideashubchelmsford.org
- Find them on Facebook: IdeasHubChelmsford
- Follow them on Twitter @IdeasHubChelms

What kind of
culture does your
brand nurture?

SAM MORRIS, SAM MORRIS COW ART

Name of business: Sam Morris Cow Art
Founder: Sam Morris
Years in business: Since 2011
Speciality: Cow art
Location: Twyning, Gloucestershire
Reach: International
Key to success: Constantly impressing your clients
Biggest challenge for businesses: Knowing where to start
Greatest asset: Can-do attitude

MAKING ART WORK

Leader in the field

Cow artist. How's that for an opening line of a conversation!

What else do you really need to hook an audience? Not much, I should think. When you have a speciality, and one as unusual as this, all you can say is *"do tell me more!"*

This is an intriguing beginning to an enthralling tale of who I now know is a woman of renaissance – bringing the art to the modern world.

It all began with Vanessa, a cow she portrayed as a gift for a friend. She enjoyed the subject and the process, but what really made it an *"a-ha"* moment was the reaction of that friend.

Happiness, elation, delight. Sam wanted to replicate the outcome and she turned it into a business.

It's not as bizarre as it may seem. After all, animal portraiture is not a new thing. Award-winning specimens have been immortalised in paintings over centuries. However, every artist does it their own way, yet not every artist can make a living out of their art. Sam Morris challenges the concept of art not being compatible with business.

Making art work

She understands that creativity is not enough to make it in business. When it comes to planning and marketing her art, she uses the Pareto Principle[1] – 20% of the year to create and 80% of time to promote and sell it. She keeps her audience close and knows their habits. Understanding how their calendar works was key to developing her business model. Summer is a season of animal fairs and exhibitions, ideal to display her artwork and get new business from cattle enthusiasts and farmers wishing to celebrate their award-winning specimens. During this time it is 80% promotion, 20% creation. This is reversed during the winter months, where online sales plays the first fiddle. It is a formula that works.

She goes one step further. She has got a plan to open what is essentially an art-themed business academy. It is for artists who want to commit to their craft full time. It took Sam three years to complete that same transition process and now she wants to teach others how to make it faster and lasting. It is about teaching them how to make a good living and develop their craft by design without relying on a middleman.

She advocates having a close relationship with the client who commissions your art. When you work for an agent, you are essentially disconnected from your inspiration and it is all about conveying that emotion.

To win you only have to be better than yourself

There were comments suggesting that she may be creating her own

1   According to Wikipedia: *"the Pareto principle (also known as the 80/20 rule, the law of the vital few, or the principle of factor sparsity) states that, for many events, roughly 80% of the effects come from 20% of the causes." (...) named after Italian economist Vilfredo Pareto, who noted the 80/20 connection while at the University of Lausanne in 1896, as published in his first paper, "Cours d'économie politique". (...) Pareto developed the principle by observing that about 20% of the peapods in his garden contained 80% of the peas."*

future competitors, but her answer to that argument is brilliant: we all do it our way.

We all have to only be our best selves to impress a client. Then the challenge is to impress them again. It is a new perspective to competition – essentially getting rid of competition by making the whole industry work in unison. Genius! I truly believe that is a great way of doing business, in any industry where direct relations with the customer can be built. Love it.

WHY A BRAND HERO?
She knows what she wants to achieve. She is an artist, yet she's methodical about her business. Her knowledge about the requirements and habits of the target market (of both business-to-business and business-to-client activities) is excellent.

In addition, Sam tries new channels of communication and does not allow her own doubts to impede her actions. She is going with *"perfectly imperfect"*[2]– the key is that she's doing it.

But what I am most impressed by is that she does not want to be the second Albrecht Dührer or George Stubbs.

She is the first Sam Morris.

MY LESSONS FROM THIS CONVERSATION
1. Find a network of peers that you will feel comfortable enough with to bounce your ideas around with
2. Choose your speciality and let it lead you
3. Tomorrow you only have to be better than yourself today

ELEMENTS OF A STRONG BRAND
- **DESIRE TO BETTER THEMSELVES**
- **KNOWLEDGE OF THE AUDIENCE**
- **AUTHENTICITY**

INSPIRATION
The Fire Starter Sessions by Danielle LaPorte, for a great approach to creative businesses and goal setting.

....
2   Refer to Sam's blog for more information on "perfectly imperfect".

MOTTO

"You don't have to be better than anybody else, just better than you thought you ever could be."

FIND OUT MORE

- Visit the website samantha-morris.com
- Follow them on Twitter @sammorriscowart
- Find them on Facebook facebook.com/SamMorrisCowArt

Which activities add up to the most powerful 20% in your brand's arsenal?

TARA PERLAKI, THE FEMININE SPACE

Name of business: The Feminine Space
Founder: Tara Perlaki
Years in business: Since 2015
Speciality: Education and consultancy focused on fertility, periods and femininity
Location: Colchester
Reach: South East England
Key to success: Understanding your flow
Biggest challenge for businesses: Understanding their flow
Greatest asset: Knowledge, support network and resolve

BEING HUMAN

The Feminine Space came about from Tara's personal need to find answers about her own health, specifically fertility and menstrual cycle. She found that, most often (even among women and medically trained staff), people's reactions to those subjects could be classified into two types: a) Bite your teeth and push through b) The woo-woo *poor you* attitude. Tara wanted answers, pointers, actions leading to improving her health. Months of search turned into years. Half of the population has periods. Surely, this area should be well researched and knowledge about the process should be common.
Well, it is not.

And this is where Tara and her Feminine Space come in.

Taboo, boo

Misconceptions, perceptions, shame, tradition are but a few minefields contaminating this subject. By sharing what she has discovered about femininity (physical and emotional aspects included) Tara dispels the myths. She is all about facts and practical outcomes, honest conversations and chasing the overwhelm women often put themselves under. She champions knowledge of self. She wants women to become more effective through their femininity, not against it. She helps them become more confident in who they are by understanding about who they are, and this means knowing what processes are taking place within their bodies.

And yes, this means saying *period, bleed, flow* and *vagina* out loud and with respect, but not without a sense of humour.

Go to The Feminine Space's Facebook page and see Tara's plush purple uterus, you will know what I mean.

Strong by being vulnerable

Tara created The Feminine Space to be a safe platform for women to figure their physiques and psyche out. And, to help them open up about it. She encourages them by sharing her own example: creating courses dedicated to flow and fertility (often in partnership with medical professionals), filming videos about the phases of the menstrual cycle, writing blogs about being (at times) *"bat shit crazy"* and why it is OK, and how to use it to your advantage. She once found herself helpless against her own health and lack of information – Tara had the guts to change it. She not only did it – does it – for herself, but she has the strength to open up and share it with other people. She is developing a community, an enlightened females' movement.

A constructive feminist

It would be very easy, given the subject, to become a confrontational business brand with an aggressive tone of voice. On the other end of the spectrum lies the possibility of becoming twee, giggly and cutesy. Tara was very careful about it and chose a more elegant, subtle way. Her brand of feminism is one that appeals to me. It is humanism, actually. She promotes respect, understanding and compassion. Tara does not want to *put men in their place*, nor is she about to burn brassieres. She wants women to be as feminine as they want to be – and for them to be able to explain what that femininity means to men. After all, most of them have never been women, so how can they know what women are going through?

So she wants both sexes to live more harmonious, happier lives – how is that for a business mission!

WHY A BRAND HERO?

As a personal brand, by sharing her own experience and being so gentle about it, she opens a path for others to follow. She tackles a difficult subject and normalises it, changing *this which must not be named* into a topic of enlightened discussion.

As a business brand, it still feels personal – she embraces her clients, with understanding, no judgement.

As a business founder, Tara went through a transition of having an idea, a very personal project, to opening it up to a wider public. It was difficult, for that was her baby, and inviting other people into it felt almost like giving it away. She did it because that was the only way to scale it up and for the project to reach its potential. Today, she is well under way to achieving her goals. With the same, if not greater, amount of care.

Also, Tara gives women courage that in itself would be enough to make her my hero.

MY LESSONS

1. Be brave in focusing on what really matters to you: your passion will help you in the process of building and maintaining your market
2. Be brave in your actions: when you go for it, go with all your might
3. Be brave in respecting your body: health matters; in order to pour energy into your business brand you need to build it up, so respect your quiet moments and recharge; understanding the flow will help you build the momentum

ELEMENTS OF A STRONG BRAND

- **RESPECT**
- **BEING OPEN TO A CONVERSATION**
- **CONFIDENCE**

INSPIRATION

- *The Optimized Woman, Using Your Menstrual Cycle to Achieve Success and Fulfillment* by Miranda Gray
- *Dance Your Way to the Top!* by Susie Heath

MOTTO
"If your compassion does not include yourself, it is incomplete" ~ Buddha

FIND OUT MORE
- Visit thefemininespace.com
- Like and follow them up on Facebook facebook.com/thefemininespace and visit their group *Connect to Your Feminine Flow*
- Follow them on Twitter @femininespace
- Subscribe to The Feminine Space YouTube channel

What type of conversations does your brand encourage?

DAME ZANDRA RHODES, ZANDRA RHODES ENTERPRISES

Name of business: Zandra Rhodes Enterprises
Founder: Dame Zandra Rhodes
Years in business: Zandra Rhodes Enterprises was incorporated in 1994 but Zandra Rhodes opened her first shop in 1967[1]
Speciality: Fashion and textiles
Location: Londonr
Reach: International
Key to success: Go on
Biggest challenge for businesses: Managing people from a distance
Greatest asset: Creativity

REALM OF A DAME

We first met at the penthouse where I've had the pleasure of being one of the guests at the intimate, but all the more impressive, evening showcasing some of Zandra Rhodes' gowns, as well as those of hand-picked guests, including nightwear and jewellery. I left that night with a few prints of her designs for theatre, a signature clutch and an amazing impression of the designer herself.

She is a signature piece, a statement, an unforgettable personal brand. She agreed to share a few thoughts about fashion and business and here's a recap of these two conversations.

This interview took place in her workshop. When I arrive she's just about to finish a Skype conference about a show and another interviewer is due in a few minutes. Even so, she decides to fit me in and for that moment her attention is undivided.

[1]   The Fulham Road Clothes Shop in London with Sylvia Ayton. Source: www.zandrarhodes.com/biography

Defining presence

The conversation was the shortest one in the series and one of the richest at the same time. Zandra Rhodes does not waste time. Leading as busy a life as hers would leave many distracted, but when asked a question, she is focused and sharp, down to a point, clever and precise. Her language is elegant, without lengthy bridges or metaphors. She says how she sees it, and that's that. It's hard to be ambiguous around her, this persona makes you make a statement and one that matters.

And the designs are the same. Defined and defining, inspiring reaction, crushing the vague.

We are surrounded by mannequins, drawings, templates, and the team is bustling around; to the untrained eye this is chaos, but only a few moments in and patterns appear. All elements have their place. They are buzzing with purpose. There is something youthful and purposeful in this place. I could spend the whole day there, just watching. Everyone being nice, smiling and making good coffee makes it a very pleasant vision indeed.

I can easily imagine people wanting to perform well in this studio, and then become even better.

WHY A BRAND HERO?
Zandra Rhodes creates designs unmistakably Zandra Rhodes. She provokes conversation that motivates viewers to seek what they are after in fashion and style. She's a pink beacon of self-expression. Respectful to self, pushing boundaries, doing what she believes is right. I left her studio feeling encouraged, feeling braver, with a great sense of respect towards the designer and Zandra Rhodes Enterprises.

MY LESSONS FROM THIS CONVERSATION
1. On fashion
She does not see herself doing anything else. You have to wear what you are creating, otherwise you are answering the wrong questions. If you are not willing to wear your own creations, who else will?

Fashion and textiles was the channel for her creativity. If then you can see somebody else wearing your garments, that always gives you pleasure.

2. On inspiration

There are many great and fabulous creators out there. But what good does it do if we were to do what they do? That's already been done. To admire and inspire is all well, but the key is to find your own way of making and creating.

3. On being the face of the brand

You can't hide. So if you want to do it, do it, but be aware that you are linking the brand to your own persona as it's you who is going to be representing it. Yes, you are at the helm, you are the frontman/woman. In this case you are the brand. Always.

ELEMENTS OF A STRONG BRAND
- CREATIVITY
- VISIBILITY
- GOOD GUESSES ABOUT WHAT CLIENTS WANT

FIND OUT MORE
- Visit zandrarhodes.com
- Visit zandrarhodes.ucreative.ac.uk

What kind of a trend does your brand inspire?

JIM ROKOS, ROKOS

Name of business: ROKOS
Founder: Jim Rokos
Years in business: Since 2011
Speciality: *"Playful, sculptural objects that behave in unexpected ways"*
Location: London
Reach: International
Key to success: Relationships and outsourcing
Biggest challenge for businesses: Route to market and finding right manufacturers
Greatest asset: Network and creativity

TELL A STORY, SURPRISE, EXCEED EXPECTATIONS

It is a rainy Thursday. The tube strike was on and off this week, so just to be safe we decided to talk via Skype. Jim is in his studio and I am in my home office. We are both surrounded by elements of our craft: samples, packaging, prototypes. It is just that in Jim's case these are samples of glass colours, packaging for his decanters and vases, and prototypes of new designs.

He is a creative director, owner and designer in his brand – developing new concepts of utilitarian art that playfully challenge the imagination of a user. They behave in an unexpected way.

The story so far

"When I was a kid I'd look at things you buy in shops and I'd always sort of thought it would be quite easy just to come up with an idea and get it produced and make a living that way. Then I forgot all about it, life took its own path. But, I seem to have come back to it much, much later on. And it is tremendously much more difficult than I'd imagined as a kid," says Jim

Rokos. Still, it is worth it.

At school, Jim favoured arts; 3D was his thing. After school, he worked in the film industry as a model maker. However, working from drawings, he found that it did not offer the opportunity to imagine his own ideas. He went on to work as an extra and a photographer's assistant, and he became a support teacher. Still on the creative side of things, but in various configurations. Then he got an MA in Product Design, which gave him an opportunity to brush up on the technical side of the process and developed his love for conceptualising ideas. This focus on theatrical and imaginative products made him *too risky to employ*, as design companies look more favourably on applicants with portfolios filled with designs that are similar to their own output. I am suspecting it turned out for the best as Jim does not strike me as a character who would be content having to create more of the same thing for too long.

So, he began his own brand.

Think about yourself as a brand

When I ask Jim about the brand, he starts reminiscing about visual elements of his identity. He says he needed a logo; he needed to look like a brand, not just a lone designer, to become more credible in the buyers' eyes.

He was lucky to have asked the right graphic designer for help. He needed a logo and approached a friend – what she did was brilliant – they mapped Jim's work, identifying what was luxury, everyday, conceptual, practical...

Then he said this: *"You really need to focus. If you are doing all those different things it's confusing to people, they won't know how to place you."* Gold.

That is what it is about. He chose a group of products, identified their traits and visualised the brand. Look at the logo: sleek, crisp, a little surprising. Not shocking, the name is clearly readable, but it makes an impression that it hides a little more than meets the eye. This is true for the products as well as the customer experience.

Tell a story

ROKOS's items are visually stunning. Each unit is perfectly executed, there are no compromises. Again, this makes developing a relationship with the manufacturers crucial and a bit tricky, as ROKOS produces small orders that nonetheless have to be of exceptional quality.

Jim strongly believes in building close relationships with suppliers and manufacturers, accrediting them with part of the success of the brand and definitely with the sleekness of the product. He appreciates their skill and experience. Jim designs the items, but they are creating them together and it's a bond full of respect.

Then there are additional touches, such as the logo on the decanters that is engraved by hand. These are examples of utilitarian art, they serve a purpose; decanters and vases are performing their duties exceptionally well. Each also tells a story. Decanters are susceptible to the influence of their content and vases bow down when the flower gets thirsty. It's very romantic.

Stay ROKOS

We talked about how small businesses can compete with big suppliers, especially in the artisan world – they are more flexible and can access people with a desirable skillset to help with promotion. Having an online shop reduces overheads; however, showcasing products in the real world is beneficial. It can be arranged through certain clients and partnerships; for example, ROKOS items are often used by high-end fashion boutiques.

ROKOS is an up-and-coming brand and a developing business. Jim is already present in a few boutique shops on the high street and he is considering larger orders as well. I have been given a little sneak-peek into what's next and these are quite exciting times filled with new designs, new product lines and distribution channels. He has an agent that helps with distribution and is developing a team to increase his reach, but he plans to keep the business a lifestyle brand. Whatever his decision will be, I know Jim is planning one thing for certain – to stay ROKOS.

WHY A BRAND HERO?

His products are quite exclusive and he is very approachable and easy to talk to. Having had this conversation with him, as I see it, in the core values, he and the business are aligned. Creativity, elegance and an element of surprise are embedded in both. These elements also make the client's experience a little more beautiful.

MY LESSONS FROM THIS CONVERSATION

1. We can all do many things but not all activities have to be performed by us – if you are busy managing the accounts, you are not designing your brand's next strategic move
2. Build relationships with your business partners and suppliers, this bond will make it easier to find better solutions and overcome crises
3. Exceed expectations, create a brand experience that leaves your clients on a high

I found out that ROKOS decanters are made with science glass, which is both excellent and extraordinary – relentless commitment to quality.

ELEMENTS OF A STRONG BRAND

- **CREATIVITY**
- **EXPERIENCE**
- **ENGAGEMENT**

INSPIRATION

If you like ROKOS, you may want to know more about Paul Smith.

MOTTO

Jim says he does not have one as such, but I picked up on a few things during our conversation that I believe have their place in this paragraph: *"Don't get distracted"*, *"Find your inspiration, find the suppliers, build relationships and use your tools to improve people's lives"*. Including your own.

DISCOVER MORE

- Visit their website rokos.co.uk
- Follow them on Instagram instagram.com/rokosdesign
- Tweet @ROKOSdesign
- Find them on Facebook facebook.com/RokosDesign

How does your brand interact with your clients?

SHAMIL SHARSHEK, LA LA PIANO BAR

Name of business: La La Piano Bar
Founders: Shamil Sharshek and David Roper
Years in business: Since 2014
Speciality: Event management (personalised live entertainment with New York piano bar quality)
Location: London
Reach: National (especially Brighton, Leeds, Manchester)
Key to success: Not giving in, learning from your mistakes and staying in touch with your audience
Biggest challenge for businesses: Funding
Greatest asset: Unique product & great partnership

MAKING THE WORLD SING ALONG

La La Piano Bar is not your typical pub with a piano in the corner and a solo pianist sitting at a keyboard, hiding behind a notice *"Don't shoot the pianist"*.

It is not karaoke either, where you are given a microphone and are left to your own devices, alone on a stage, trying to hit a note. La La is all about lights and action, engagement, letting your hair down, letting loose, taking in the ambiance. Their events engage multiple performers and are vibrant, full of boa feathers and live music as well as singalongs. It is a concept realised in a unique way. There is nothing else like this in London, and perhaps even in the whole of Britain. Shamil and David are on a mission to change this state of affairs.

1 + 1 = 11

Putting La La in every city in the UK is their goal. They are starting with London, creating open La La nights once a month. These events are a chance for the public to see what they are really capable of – La La is a serious events company.

In Shamil's own words: *"La La Piano Bar have entertained for various big birthdays, special events such as Waterstones' Christmas party, and the 1930s-themed night for the celebration of the Simpson building.*

We also played at the Winterville festival in 2015 in the world famous Spiegeltent. This is in addition to over 20 public events at the top venues in London and around the UK.

We partnered with Business against Poverty and raised substantial amounts for BAP and Cancer Research.

Then, in March 2017, La La Piano Bar entered the international corporate events stage with our first event, for a large software company at the Mobile World Congress in Barcelona.

We also entertained at several festivals, such as the Brighton Fringe, Brockley Max and Telegraph Hill, and proved the concept can work anywhere - as our bespoke live entertainment and singalongs appeal to everyone, whatever their background."

David Roper is the soul behind the creative development and Shamil Sharshek watches over the business side of things. It is a great partnership as they have very different skills, and are aware and respectful of each other's skills and talents.

David has the show business know how, having been a quarter of the *4 Poofs and a Piano*, livening up *Friday Night with Jonathan Ross* for nine years. Shamil has experience in project management and business development. This combination propels La La forward.

Delivering to many through personalised experience

Today, apart from organising La La nights, they also manage private bookings – book launches, private parties, corporate anniversaries. They have got so far thanks to self-funding and resourcefulness. But there's only so far you can get on your own. The business is definitely scalable and they are considering franchising in the future, but to get to that step they need funding. That's their next big challenge. The audience grasps La La's concept in a heartbeat. This allows them to grow organically, making success sustainable, albeit a function of time – although they may change their minds and open La La to investors.

Make space and they will come

They are growing and learning. The format works well in London and they are taking it to new audiences. It seems they are able to find their own crowd even when performing in a venue for the first time.

These are the people who look for a different style of entertainment, for a new experience. Thinking outside the box, La La will write an original song to go with the theme of your event! They will write a personal birthday song for a birthday party. All to make an event a one-off, dedicated to you. All they need is a bit of space. They have everything else – performers, music and La La atmosphere. They specialise in creating and uniting communities, even for one night, as after a few songs even the shy sing along. *"There is something special about the whole room singing together,"* says Shamil. La La makes it happen.

WHY A BRAND HERO?

They are on the way to make the world sing along. *"Let's start with the UK,"* smiles Shamil. To me, that is a great mission to have. The spirit of La La really comes alive during the events and they are doing a good job of making the essence of their brand evident across various communication platforms, and with good strength. They make themselves visible and memorable for all the right reasons. They are gaining momentum and show no signs of stopping. And, in whichever way you meet them – via social media or in person – they make it easy for you to join in and become a part of La La Piano Bar. That is why they are my brand hero.

MY LESSONS
1. Keep at it, even if the success does not come straight away
2. It's hard work, be prepared for it
3. Having long-term goals will help you overcome issues on the way, find ways to innovate and keep moving

ELEMENTS OF A STRONG BRAND
- **LEARNING FROM YOUR OWN MISTAKES**
- **ABILITY TO GROW**
- **CLARITY**

INSPIRATION
Richard Branson's biography, because he is open about the ups and downs of business. In addition, Branson's involved in so many things, and that's entrepreneurship: having ideas, developing them, not necessarily keeping to one industry, one business. But, whatever he does, he has a vision, and it is clear through all of his endeavours.

MOTTO
Shamil did not verbalise one as such, but it seems to me that it could say: *"When you're down, stand up, adapt and go on."*

FIND OUT MORE
- Visit their website lalapianobar.com
- Follow them on Twitter @lalapianobar
- Find them on Facebook facebook.com/LalaPianoBar

How strong is your brand's presence across platforms?

MAŁGORZATA SKIBIŃSKA, BO WARTO[1]

Name of business: Bo Warto, social and cultural news platform
Founder: Małgorzata Skibińska
Years in business: Since 2017
Speciality: Finding and promoting stories with a positive impact
Location: London
Reach: National
Key to success: Determination
Biggest challenge for businesses: Not doubting yourself and taking the plunge
Greatest asset: Network

GOOD NEWS, GOOD TO READ

Truth be told I cannot remember when I first met Gosia[2]. Feels like she has always been there, somewhere, ever present in the peripheries of my mind. She has that effect on people, I found; being a reliable constant in their lives.

It was one of the evening meetings of Polish Professionals in London, a society uniting, as the name suggests, professionals of various denominations, all with Polish ancestry. Gosia was the chair of the board at the time and it was very important to her to be the one to meet all newcomers, interview them diligently and immediately connect them to individuals with whom they would have a shared interest.

---

1   Polish: *Because it's worth it*

2   *Gosia* (pronounce *Gosha*) is a short form of *Małgorzata*

The last girl scout[3]

Gosia, I will have you know, seems to be acquainted with everyone; or, at the very least, connected to someone who knows that person of interest really well. She is a relentless talent connector, human passions and business-interest joiner. She thrives in linking good people with decent opportunities and in connecting good people together.

She is also, always and forever, a girl scout, who always puts the good of others before her own. Those who knew her could not wait to see Gosia benefit from her powers herself. Finally, in 2017 with the portal Bo Warto, she did it.

Of quality or not at all

Bo Warto is a news portal for social and cultural stories of interest to the Polish community within the UK. It is not just another online bulletin board. It an online magazine with a purpose; the purpose to share quality stories about people, events, and achievements – of quality.

It is a bigger challenge to engage readers in a story of a sensational profile. To scare, shock or disgust with a view to cash in on clicks would be, according to Gosia, a waste of effort. A good story needs to have substance and elegant form. It needs to be rooted within the community's spirit and touch on their current passions and future aspirations. It is essential for it to be well crafted as well. Gosia would know, as she is a journalist with a MA in International Relations and a ministerial medal awarded for her achievements as a columnist.

She chooses subjects that enlighten, teach, inspire and bring people together. Bo Warto was founded to lift people up, to show them that quality is achievable and reachable, and that we all can be a part of it.

Becoming a leader

Gosia is an idealist. An independent woman. A strong personality who is used to organising things for others. She knows how to

3   *Girl guide* is the proper term; however, I am using this with a reference to Tony Scott's movie The Last Boy Scout. It is an Americanism, I understand, but in this context it sounds better to me.

generate content of quality, and compromise has never been an option. Yet, striving for perfection had been taking too long. Gosia faced a choice: doing everything and learning on the way, or engaging others. Not being a programmer herself, she needed help – that was something she was not used to. Changing that mindset paid off. Although it came as a little surprise: she did not have to do everything on her own – and no one expected her to! It was a change from being the only one in this project to becoming a leader of this venture.

Not good enough for too long

Gosia allowed herself to give up on not being good enough. It is very liberating to be as close to perfection as we are today. I know it was a big decision for her. She always wanted to give her portal the best possible start. However, no matter how good it is in the beginning – there will always be room for improvement. Because users will discover a better navigational sequence… because of the software updates… there are always more of those 'becauses'.

Those two elements: becoming a leader and being good enough, is what made it possible for Bo Warto to be introduced to its readers. Readers who waited for it. Wanted it. Readers who appreciate how good it already is and enjoy it becoming better.

Good things to come

Although publishing the portal was a pivotal event in the brand's timeline, it was a stage nonetheless. Now is a time of growing readership, increasing influence and testing. Her methodology encompasses three steps: information, integration, social innovation.

Bo Warto has ambitions of becoming a benchmark of quality within the community. It will always be there to spread the word about what matters to the community. Watch this space – it is worth it.

WHY A BRAND HERO?
This portal gives me hope that TED[4] talks with their ideas worth

4   To find out more about TED talks, visit TED.com TED is a nonprofit organisation dedicated to promoting "ideas worth spreading", in a form of short videos. TED began in 1984 as a conference and has been held annually since 1990. Today you can find their stories touch on almost all aspects of life and in over 100 languages.

sharing and projects such as People of New York are not just a trend, but a movement. Uplifting stories, perhaps due to their gentler nature, do not find a following as easily. Gosia makes a space for good news and lifts people up. For that, she is my brand hero.

MY LESSONS
1. Define *a good enough* stage to go to market and/or publish content about your brand (make it as good as can be); allow yourself not to be perfect as becoming such takes too long to make sense on the market
2. Knowing that your products and/or services may need to be improved in the future does not mean they are bad at the moment; it just means you are prepared to listen to your audience and offer a better service
3. Believe in people and find those who believe in you

ELEMENTS OF A STRONG BRAND
- QUALITY OF CONTENT
- QUALITY OF PRESENTATION
- QUALITY OF ACTIONS: AT LEAST A PORTION OF OUR ACTIONS NEEDS TO BENEFIT SOCIETY

INSPIRATION
- humansofnewyork.com

MOTTO
"Only truth is interesting" ~ *Józef Mackiewicz*

FIND OUT MORE
- Visit bowartoorg.uk
- Go to facebook.com/Bo-Warto
- Find Gosia on LinkedIn (search for Małgorzata Skibińska)

How does your brand benefit the society?

....

....

....

....

....

NATASHA SPENCER, LION SPIRIT MEDIA

Name of business: Lion Spirit Media
Founder: Natasha Spencer
Years in business: Since February 2015
Speciality: Marketing and PR strategy and implementation
Location: Hampshire
Reach: South East
Key to success: Relationships and outsourcing
Biggest challenge for businesses: Perseverance and resilience – failure is all part of the journey
Greatest asset: Knowledge

SHOWING BUSINESSES HOW TO TALK TO PEOPLE

I met Natasha at a social media training course I joined to refresh my knowledge and reinvigorate my online profile. She was teaching. A journalist with a law background creating her own writing consultancy. This combination intrigued me, so I invited her for a conversation to find out what her business mission is and why she is a copywriter different from all others.

She can write about everything from sociology to biology; she is a journalist, she knows her craft. But she has one more asset, one that is not so common among writers – a BA in Law.

It stood out to me that this is her strongest selling point and not a bad differentiator.

Legal aid

So what is Natasha's mission? To help businesses find their *roar*. To change the way industries communicate. She is still a blogger and a journalist using her skills *"to maximise [client's] business potential and financial benefit through the correct use of social media, internet services and creative marketing"* – using her legal knowledge and technical editorial experience to focus on the legal and financial sector as one of her core industries. The plan is to concentrate on translating all the legalese into plain English in order to make this line of work more accessible to young people. To show them the true colours of these industries, make them more open and inviting.

Increasing clarity in the way these two communicate is no mean feat, as they are known for the love of long words and complex phrases. I am glad someone has the idea to rework this system. The less corporates hide behind problematical phraseology, the better. And I can see people supporting this idea. I myself am looking forward to the day all businesses are on the same page with their clients – that's part of Inc Element's branding mission.

Law in order

Natasha is a young brand, but already one that is aware that choosing a speciality does not mean letting go of your other advantages. It just helps make your messages stronger and avoids confusion with your target market. The way she chose to do it is by creating a sub brand specialising in providing copywriting services to legal and financial business. The other sub brand is going to focus on more general subjects. The division keeps the attention undiluted and creates two lines of business, potentially increasing the power with which both can penetrate their markets. I think it's a very smart move and I am looking forward to seeing how she translates it to her online and offline communication.

WHY A BRAND HERO?

To some extent it is easier to say that *"we do everything"*, especially when you are not selling a physical product you have to put on the shelves of your shop. When you know your craft, you can use your abilities to write on almost every subject. Businesses often start that way to maintain cash flow. It takes courage to choose your identity and Natasha is making that move early in her entrepreneurial journey, which in my mind is the first stage of becoming a strong brand.

MY LESSONS FROM THIS CONVERSATION
1. Letting go of the 'everything' pays off in the long run
2. Defining yourself helps you stand out
3. It also guides your brand's development

ELEMENTS OF A STRONG BRAND
- CLARITY OF COMMUNICATION
- FOCUS ON SPECIALISATION
- PASSION

INSPIRATION
Apple, the business, the brand, the product, for their story of ups and downs

MOTTO
"Have a vision. Have a foresight. Find your Roar."

FIND OUT MORE
- Visit her LinkedIn profile /in/natashaspencer
- Follow her on Twitter @lionspiritmedia

What is your brand's communication style?

HIROMI STONE, KINOMI

Name of business: Kinomi
Founder: Hiromi Stone
Years in business: Since 2010
Speciality: Mixed nuts rich with umami
Location: London
Reach: Local
Key to success: Satisfaction coming from being close to the client
Biggest challenge for businesses: Not acting like a business
Greatest asset: The product and philosophy of taste

THE FIFTH ELEMENT

"I want to introduce you to a super lady, founder of a snack nut company called Kinomi. She is a Japanese lady living in London who created this nut company out of repeated requests from her cooking students. Her name is Hiromi Stone."

This is how Hiromi was introduced to me and I think to quote this message is the best way of introducing this Brand Hero. When I read it I knew I was in for something good. When I looked at Hiromi's website I realised that this is going to be even better.

Another dimension

4D cinema is happening, with shaking seats, bubbles and aromas. Perhaps technology in the future will enable us to experience 4D websites. Today I can tell you that what Hiromi created with her brand is not far off already. You can almost taste her product with your eyes. It's luscious, vibrant, moreish. It's more than you expect. It's an all-engaging experience. A type of grown-up ball pit of a brand – joy all round.

It all began in Hiromi's kitchen.

The discovery

Cookery school was Hiromi's way of fitting a business around her life. Her home was the school's HQ and, as the lessons were held in the evenings, she needed something for her students to snack on, so she would prepare her own eats: nuts with sake, soy sauce and kombu. The cooking was all about umami, the fifth taste that makes you go *ummmm*. The nut mixes had that in abundance, so people started asking for it, and she would prepare a bespoke combination, as requested. Then Hiromi went to Ms Marmite Lover's flat-based farmer's market and met a distributor… and this is how it started. However, even with her first client being Harvey Nichols, she still did not really think about the business side too much. *"That [the business] wasn't the part that I liked,"* admits Hiromi.

Cracking the nut

Still, it was a success and orders followed. Soon the demand for nuts made it impossible for Hiromi to continue the cookery school as she was roasting day and night, packing 60 kilograms of nuts per week. That was when she realised she needed to find a supplier to help her cope with all the requests for the product. Around that time another thought appeared as well – this is a business, even if she was still very much focusing on preparing and packaging the product. Order-wise, it was a sinusoid with periods of very high intensity and quiet time intertwined. Hiromi realised that to make sense of it all it was necessary for her to step out of the kitchen and analyse the wider perspective. This was a decision that began the sustainable growth of her brand.

Hiromi does not follow recipes, she creates her own

She has a very clear idea of where she wants to be. *"I want to be the standard against which the quality of other nut-based products is measured"* – how is that for a mission, ladies and gentlemen! She is not going to stop there as Hiromi wants to make sure quality control in the nut industry is being observed 360°. That means quality and an ethical approach across the board: for the farmers and pickers, making sure the land on which nuts are being grown is being ethically managed... Then there is also an additional possibility – improving the taste of the *free from* range of food. Hiromi herself is dairy-free and cannot eat wheat. That does not stop her from being a connoisseur. When your choices are limited, you have more reasons to appreciate what you can eat. She simply will not stand for *bland*, where *delicious* is a possibility. Actually, that she has already started, because all Kinomi products have what its creator calls a *sneaky health element*, but the taste must be there to make a product really good for you.

It is a quest that grabs my imagination. Plus, the product is super-tasty (so says my husband, who emptied the packet of cardamom nuts I was presented with... I will just have to get another one to confirm his findings). Hiromi still states she's not a business person. But she is getting there. She is doing this with the help of Cinnamon Bridge, Food and Beverage Accelerator. She has a great product and they are helping her with business strategies to make it the success it deserves to be.

WHY A BRAND HERO?

Japanese cuisine is geared towards not spoiling nature's riches. It's about making quality ingredients stand out. *"Even in the complex dishes you can still identify and appreciate the ingredients,"* says Hiromi.

This appreciation is what Kinomi is all about. Simple ingredients beautifully combined. You can taste it even by looking at her website. That, to me, is a fantastic start for a brand. She says she only thought of the name when the packaging manufacturer asked her what to put on the label. She chose Kinomi, which is Japanese for nut. No unnecessary embellishments. Perfect. Hiromi has great plans for her brand; she wants to change the world – as, I think, every true brand should want to do in some respect. I believe with every fibre of my being that she is going to do the impossible, and that makes her mighty.

ELEMENTS OF A STRONG BRAND
- **TASTE**
- **CLARITY**
- **IT SHOULD MAKE YOU SAY** *"MMM"*

MY LESSONS

1. Appreciate your heritage, it can become your greatest strength
2. Being a strong business is a necessary element of a strong brand
3. Do not go it alone, find support in the areas that are not your expertise

MOTTO

"There's no point, if it doesn't taste good."

DISCOVER MORE

- Visit kinominuts.com
- Find them on Facebook @KinomiByHiromiStone
- Follow them on Twitter @KinomiNuts
- Look them up on Instagram kinominuts

What new dimensions does your brand explore?

VANESSA STRAUSS, BRIGHT FOX LETTINGS

Name of business: Bright Fox Lettings
Founder: Vanessa Strauss
Years in business: Since 2012
Speciality: Creating an ecosystem for thriving evolution of landlords and tenants
Location: Royal Tunbridge Wells
Reach: Local
Key to success: Keep doing the right thing
Biggest challenge for businesses: Getting disengaged and sacrificing their values for the sake of a quick income
Greatest asset: Clients and the business's honesty

HOLD YOUR NERVE

"Vanessa has a lettings agency that creates an ecosystem for landlords and tenants to thrive in." This is how she was introduced to me by a mutual friend. I was hooked, wanted to find out more and agreed that she sounds like an excellent fit for the Brand Heroes project.

As Vanessa is based close to the border of East Sussex, we agreed Skype would be the most prudent medium for our interview. We agreed to an early morning session, 8am. Vanessa in her office (no clutter, just orderly, bright space) and me at my desk. She is witty, open and very professional, with clearly defined values and vision for the brand. This is the summary of our conversation.

I kick the conversation off with a question about the past – it is always interesting for me to find out whether an entrepreneur has had any previous business experience and what had influenced them to take this plunge and launch the brand in question.

In this case, it all grew from an unsatisfactory client experience.

Both her husband and Vanessa had properties in and around Tunbridge Wells and their experience as landlords had been poor: communication left a lot to be desired, properties were mismanaged, assets were not looked after and neither were the tenants. Vanessa noticed the insufficiencies and pain points for both homeowners and tenants.

Bright Fox began as a small business with a mission to create best practice.

First point of call: research. Proper research. They investigated what displeased people about letting or renting their property, what was painful about the process, the preparation of the property and the aftercare. This knowledge was the basis on which Vanessa developed Bright Fox's ethos and their business model grew from that.

So, what are they about? *"Creating a very equal, open, honest, communicative model where everyone felt valued, people were looked after, and went back to the fundamentals of building trusting relationships that would then turn into successful long-term business relationships,"* says Vanessa.

It began as a way of solving a situation that by many had been seen as a necessary evil, and then it grew into creating something optimistic and good.

I am fascinated by the idea of creating an ecosystem. It is only logical. But it comes straight from the heart. Bright Fox develop an understanding with the stakeholder – a homeowner, a tenant – of what they want and what they deem important, then tailor their services to their needs.

They appreciate that relationship is a two-way construct. Hence, they are making the step towards their clients. They treat them as business partners. This is audible and visible across the brand.

At Bright Fox, a landlord is a homeowner, a tenant is looking to make a home. It may be a subtle distinction, but it is potent and influences the relationships between the parties.

The colours and symbols of the brand are clear and vibrant, defined and well composed. Fox was chosen as an agile, nimble, adaptable animal – as these qualities need to be reflected in this brand as well.

In an industry that is dominated by faceless chains and struggling boutique agencies that compete on price, Vanessa decided to create a space for relationships.

"After all, a home and keeping promises are emotional things."
~ Vanessa Strauss

I suspect that may be why her business is doing better and better, growing through referrals. She wants to keep tweaking it and adjusting to her clients' needs and develop it further according to her brand values. That means cooperating with people that share them – each potential team member gets a business plan to read prior to any engagement. Brave and shrewd. Then again, that is Bright Fox Lettings.

WHY A BRAND HERO?
The ecosystem idea is an ingenious one – it encompasses the brand's spirit. It is the one I am always going to remember Bright Fox by and it is brilliant that they have it published on the home page of their website. There are a few other good lettings agencies out there but I've yet to come across one that stands out (for all the right reasons) as much as Vanessa's brand. From that point of view, she is a pioneer and she definitely is a champion of good brand values and entrepreneurial spirit.

Her business grows organically. She is prepared to hold her nerve throughout the process and this gives her time to make her brand even stronger and she does it by design. For that I take my hat off to her, as this is why Bright Fox Lettings is my brand hero.

MY LESSONS FROM THIS CONVERSATION
1. Do not compromise your values for the sake of a quick income
2. Be nimble and adaptable...
3. ...but do not lose sight of the values your brand stands for

ELEMENTS OF A STRONG BRAND
- EQUALITY
- OPENNESS
- COMMUNICATIVENESS

INSPIRATION
- John Lewis, for the values he brought into the industry and creating a legacy of excellent service
- The Prince of Wales, for opening new routes to market, and championing equality and engagement between retailers and suppliers

MOTTO
"Help me help you"[1]

FIND OUT MORE
- Visit their website brightfoxlettings.co.uk
- Follow them on Twitter @TheBrightFox
- Find them on Facebook @BrightFoxLettings
- Look them up on instagram.com/BRIGHTFOXLETTINGS

What is your brand's communication style?

---

1   This is a quote from *Jerry Maguire*, a 1996 American romantic comedy-sports drama film written, produced and directed by Cameron Crowe. Vanessa proves that *"Help me help you"* has real-life applications.

EMMA STROUD, TRUTH.WORKS.

Name of business: Truth.Works.
Founders: Emma Stroud and Deon Newbronner (I am speaking with Emma)
Years in business: Truth.Works. was brought to life in 2016, but Emma – a business woman, speaker, host, performer, writer and theatre director – has been active professionally for the past 15 years
Speciality: Helping senior executives, business owners and entrepreneurs find, speak and live their truth
Location: London
Reach: International
Key to success: Communicating your truth
Biggest challenge for businesses: Using their voice the right way and being true to themselves
Greatest asset: Combined experience of founding partners and developing own IP, i.e. their truth

YOUR TRUE VOICE

The office of Truth. Works. is located in one of the London-themed hubs. Theirs is all about Alice in Wonderland. When you enter, you get the feeling of stepping out of the ordinary. A fitting environment for a brand that helps their clients see beyond the average.

When I met Emma, I thought her quest is to give people a voice and teach them to use it wisely. After all, when developed, it becomes an instrument of great power and, as such, it commands great responsibility. That is only part of the truth. In fact, what Emma and her business partner Deon do under the Truth.Works. banner is to unleash the power within their clients by helping them identify and speak their truth.

"Our work unlocks an individual's power to influence, creating wealth for them and their clients." ~ Emma Stroud

It is a sunny Monday afternoon, and we sit at a café near the headquarters of Truth.Works. on Boundary Row in London. We begin. It is our first live conversation; we never met before and yet dialogue flows freely – there is humour, wit, openness and confidence. It is easy to listen to Emma. She is an experienced award-winning comedy performer; she created sell-out shows for over 15 years – and she describes herself as having *"a passion for creating stories that provoke laughter and thought in every audience"*. When it comes to business, it is transparent that it is no laughing matter to her, as finding what really works was not a matter of overnight success.

It takes two

He is a master coach, author, speaker and human nature specialist, and she a business woman, speaker, host, performer, writer and theatre director (according to the Truth.Works. website). As business partners they are good together. Yet, perfecting that goodness did take time.

Emma and Deon decided to get to the core, and asked their clients, who came back to them with a whopper of a summary: *"Without a doubt you are brilliant at helping people become best versions of themselves."*

It seems they have been fulfilling this objective throughout their careers, through their individual activities and co-created brands.

Courage to grow

The end of 2016 was the right time for Deon and Emma to bring Truth.Works. to life. The best outlet for their talents to date.

The theme of helping their clients better themselves is stronger than ever. Truth.Works. emphasises the connection between truth and trust as the cornerstone of leadership. What I particularly like about their approach is that they describe relationship building as a hard skill. When I first read it I thought – of course that's right, yet they were the first ones I came across who say it is a misconception to approach it as a soft skill. They say it openly and so their clients know to be prepared to work hard.

Pay attention → earn trust

Telling stories is another theme in my mind irrevocably linked to Emma and Deon. Telling true stories, that is. Stories that stay with their clients, with their audiences, not only in the business context. I may not remember exactly what Emma had said during our conversation (that is why I had it recorded) but I remember clearly that she made me feel welcome, at ease and respected. We all tell stories and Truth.Works. teach clients how to pay attention to the stories, how to make them matter, how to make them last. They help their clients – senior executives, business owners and entrepreneurs – communicate their truth, which leads to connecting with their audiences' emotions, which leads to building relationships. And that is a very hard skill to learn.

Uncommon approach to common sense

"Fact is a commonly held belief. Knowledge can be questioned.
When you tell a story, no one can question it, because it's your story."
~ Emma Stroud

We all have it, yet our own truth can be an awfully hard thing to find. It is a human thing, I guess. And we all tell stories, yet Emma and Deon can teach us to do it better. They enable clients to amplify skills that they already have – by finding their truth they influence their habits and behaviours, by analysing and rebuilding their communication they create space for extraordinary leaders to emerge: leaders who tell the truth.

It's scary how uncommon that speaking our own truths has become. I am grateful that Emma and Deon are working to change that.

WHY A BRAND HERO?

I like that she calls things how they are. There is no false self-deprecation or cutesy modesty. There's honesty and nothing else is needed. Truth.Works. bring storytelling to a level it should be at. Giving people tools to get the amazing stories out of them. That grabs my imagination, that is what I want to see more of and that is why they are my brand hero.

MY LESSONS FROM THIS CONVERSATION
1. Stick to your own self, choosing someone else's character just to fit the convention won't do you any favours
2. Finding your own truth is a hard process that takes bravery and skill
3. Building relationships is a hard skill and it should be approached as such

ELEMENTS OF A STRONG BRAND
- NEED & MARKET
- PERSONALITY
- CLIENTS BEING ADVOCATES OF THE BRAND
- THEIR TRUTH

INSPIRATION
- Check officespaceintown.com, creators of spaces with a theme, for remarkable stories in architecture and excellent client service, and openness to collaboration
- Naked Wines, for the product, stories and care and being able to connect with their clients even though they only have an online presence
- Secret Escapes, for smart identification of the niche and the way they use their language, nuances (member vs visitor)
- Tesco, for clever approach to their own brand
- M&S, for the strapline

Emma performed and produced an award-winning one woman show 'Coming Out of My Box' in October 2015 to sell-out audiences in London and – at the time of writing – is preparing the return of her one woman show 'Coming Out of My Box - the Revenge', which is to be performed at the end of 2017.

MOTTO
"To help exceptional people stand out from the crowd. Be yourself and play more."

DISCOVER MORE
- Visit truth-works.co.uk
- Follow Emma on Twitter @emstroud
- Find her on LinkedIn linkedin.com/in/emma-stroud

What is your brand's truth?

CAROLINE TAPLIN, MINDFULNESS UNLTD

Name of business: Mindfulness UnLtd
Founder: Caroline Taplin MSW DipSW Cert. Recovery and Wellness Coach, HCPC (acc), SHTC (acc)
Years in business: In the industry since 1999, Mindfulness UnLtd created in 2014
Speciality: Mindfulness classes, workshops and courses in the areas of recovery, rehabilitation and stress
Location: Chelmsford
Reach: South East
Key to success: Be aware
Biggest challenge for businesses: Borrowing reserves from the next day
Greatest asset: Knowledge

BE AWARE, YOUR LIFE DEPENDS ON IT

Much appreciated

Caroline appreciates accents. Caroline appreciates moments. Caroline appreciates people. That's what mindfulness is all about. In a nutshell, mindfulness is being aware. According to Williams, Teasdale, Segal and Kabat-Zinn (2007), whom she quotes on her website, *"Mindfulness is the awareness that emerges through: paying attention; on purpose; in the present moment; non-judgementally...as if your life depended on it..."*

Caroline's goal is to (re)introduce mindfulness to schools and corporate institutions. She is at the beginning of her quest, working directly with individuals, small businesses and local authorities.

That is why I invited her for a chat (which lasted almost three hours).

We talked about the reality of social work, personal development and creating a business.

Problem, no problem

What is impressive about Caroline's business and her personally is the mission to change the way so-called social services are being delivered these days. Do not get this wrong – we both agree that these services are needed and important – but the delivery became too automatic. If recipients were not making enough progress it means it's not being done right. Actually, the service on offer may be at fault as well. By default, services have to be standardised, but the workers who deliver them should be mindful enough to be able to recognise what is needed and use a matrix of services. Not only to elevate the symptoms, but to recognise and deal with the problems.

The problem is that they themselves are not being taught how to. Caroline's on a mission to give those lone workers a proper support. Not to limit them, but to give them greater confidence and improve awareness. She believes this type of education should be made compulsory even in schools. I agree – I think it would be a valuable addition to the curriculum.

That is the future. Today, Caroline develops her own methodology and works with those who want to improve their perception of life and professional performance. She helps people recovering from addiction to set up and grow businesses and she helps struggling entrepreneurs regain their momentum. She notices who they are now and how they can build on that – without judgement and fear.

It is a valuable and rare commodity. You may say it's mere kindness. But having spent that time with Caroline, I know it's experience and knowledge with kindness. If you're moaning (she does not like moaners) but want to do something about it, OK – it's a start.

WHY A BRAND HERO
I chose this business as my brand hero because of the Herculean task they chose to tackle. Caroline does not seek awards, glory and honours. She focuses on the task at hand: this person, this class, this workshop. One at a time. Mindfully. We need more of those people, so focused on their audience, so determined to deliver change to the

whole industry.

When I read
Caroline's bio
on her website I
discovered that
she is a Cloud
Appreciation
Society member.
How mindful is
that?

MY LESSONS FROM THIS CONVERSATION
1. Be mindful of your brand
2. Be mindful of your audience
3. Be mindful of your goals

ELEMENTS OF A STRONG BRAND
- **AWARENESS**
- **MISSION**
- **QUALITY VISUAL REPRESENTATION**

MOTTO
"Mindfulness really does change your mind"

FIND OUT MORE
- Visit mindfulness-UnLtd.com
- Find Caroline's LinkedIn profile linkedin.com/in/carolinetaplin

*How mindful is
your brand?*

TRISTAN TITEUX, EMPATIKA

Name of business: Empatika
Founder: Tristan Titeux
Years in business: Since 2003
Speciality: Custom-fitted furniture with ethical pedigree
Location: London
Reach: National
Key to success: Keep at what you are good at

YOU CHOOSE WHAT YOU ARE MADE OF

Elements of creation

Furniture and food – what do they have in common? Their quality can greatly affect the quality of our lives. It counts where they come from and what implications on our environment the preparation process has. They say *"you are what you eat"*. After my conversation with Tristan I am more inclined to say that you are what you surround yourself with. That includes inanimate objects.

Tristan Titeux is a furniture designer, a mindful environmentalist, a carpenter, a peaceful warrior. He poured all these traits into his brand, bringing us bespoke, fitted eco furniture. His personal influence is shaping an impactful business identity – Empatika.

I have met Tristan a few times and he has always been super calm and very modest. He points towards his work to do the talking. His creations have a way of making quite an impression – whether it's his book, a talk or his furniture.

Furniture designer

Furniture is a category of utilitarian equipment. It needs to serve a purpose. It needs to fit within our lives to truly fulfil its role: not to be an obstacle but a complement to your daily cycle. That is why Empatika measures more than inches. They look at actual dimensions of your life before proposing another object to fill it. The *"what for..."* and *"why do you need it..."* is more important than *"Here's one I made earlier"*. It's not about putting planks together, but about creating a solution.

Mindful modernist

What I find fantastic about Empatika is that they combine a conscious approach to sustainability with an understanding of the challenges of a modern life. I guess we have Tristan's heritage to thank for that. Especially Tristan's father. He was an eccentric character – a forager who, every Sunday for about five years, had an hour slot on RTBF national radio in Belgium, where he spoke about wild plants. When Tristan told me about his childhood, he lovingly described thick stone walls of an old house, no hot water, no TV, foraging berries in the forest, tending their own goats and chickens. There was richness, honesty, wisdom and purity. No pollutants; chemicals and media kept at bay. Nowadays people pay good money to rid themselves of these contaminants. Tristan grew up surrounded by this clarity. In touch with nature and her rhythm. This lifestyle, this understanding, he includes in his business brand.

Carpenter

He is a trained carpenter. This means familiarity with the material, appreciation of the craft, knowing the limitations of the wood and an understanding of where the boundaries of the design can be pushed. Creating beautiful utilitarian eco objects is at the heart of the business. Keeping the brand in close touch with its core is a very important element of Empatika's success.

Peaceful warrior

Tristan appreciates nature. He notices its goodness and its beauty. This is not idle admiration, however; he recognises the challenge of keeping close to it without detaching yourself from a modern lifestyle. That is why, again, Empatika keeps nature at its source, creating furniture solutions fit for a lifestyle city people are accustomed to. He found a way of bringing nature back into the city. His chosen platform is beautiful furniture.

Innovator

Tristan says he has always been fascinated by how things work and fit together. He converted part of his teenage bedroom into a workshop. This interest in finding out how various materials can be combined into creating something better translated into what Empatika's creations are made of. You will find this brand to be a true innovator. What you notice at the first glance is a stunning bookcase; what you then discover is what it is made of, and that can be hemp, straw, mushroom... good for the designer, the client, and the environment of both.

Constructive environmentalist

Empatika is a brand that champions great design. That, in their ethos, includes great materials. This means ethically sourced, quality ingredients to create utilitarian pieces of art. It's not about burning all plastic, polystyrene, PVC, etc. That would create a black cloud of toxic fumes, for one. But if we develop a lifestyle that reduces the need for plastic, it will become a thing of the past. This is a strategy reintroducing nature into our daily routine without compromising the lifestyle.

They are the only company I know of that buys an acre of the rainforest for every customer who spends over £5,000; this land is bought via World Land Trust with a view to being left unspoilt for eternity. Also, in their work Empatika use 100% renewable electrical energy.

For now, the first cell of this movement is located in London. There are plans to create Empatika hubs all over the UK. The ripples of change have already been created. I personally am looking forward to seeing the wave.

WHY A BRAND HERO

New concept starts from one application

Empatika sympathises with the need for quality, designed, functional solutions that work in harmony with the environment...
- of the client: their space and rhythm of life
- of the designer: who wants to create beautiful objects fulfilling the brief and generating satisfaction for the maker

- of nature: there is a way of designing and manufacturing functional furniture preserving the future for posterity

Tristan and Empatika talk about it, write about it and implement it. However, what I believe is most important of all, they invite us to join in. It's not about feeling guilty about using not-so-eco materials, but about realising that we can choose good design and honest materials without compromising quality. Empatika makes it possible.

MY LESSONS FROM THIS CONVERSATION
1. Your business is as strong as your belief in it
2. Inclusion is stronger than exclusion
3. There are more eco solutions available than you may think

ELEMENTS OF A STRONG BRAND
- **CONFIDENCE**
- **CONSISTENCY**
- **CHARACTER**

FIND OUT MORE
- Visit empatika.uk
- Find Tristan on LinkedIn (search EMPATIKA Fitted Furniture)
- Read *Furniture for the Future: How What You Buy Can Change the World* by Tristan Titeux

I have been to his book launch and the samples of materials he exhibited are mind-blowing. For example, shelves we can grow from fungi (durable and nice to touch and not smelly, just in case you wondered).

How sympathetic is your brand - to the need of your client, to the need of the environment...

....
....
....
....
....
....
....
....
....
....
....
....
....

RICK TOOLEY, PREMIUM PRICE CONSULTANTS AND LONDON MULTILIST

Name of business: Premium Price Consultants (PPC) and London Multilist (LM)
Founders: Rick and Sandra Tooley
Years in business: Premium Price Consultants since 2015, London Multilist since 2011, and in the industry since mid nineties
Speciality: Property – achieving tomorrow's value today
Location: London
Reach: National
Key to success: Give all your ideas away, but charge for implementation
Biggest challenge for businesses: Realising that the product is 30%, maybe 25% of your success, the rest is strategy and route to market
Greatest asset: Business partner & IP

ASK FOR WHAT YOU WANT, THIS IS THE BEST WAY TO TRUE COLLABORATION

We meet at a café in central London. Rick is a relaxed gentleman with a melodic New Zealand accent. He laughs often and tells great stories, but he's dead serious about the business. Premium Price Consultants and London Multilist steadily increase their share of the British real estate market because their owners support their products with a defined strategy based on cooperation.

Having a great product helps achieve commercial success, but it does not give a guarantee. If you do not know how to achieve a proper price, when and where to market your goods, you are setting yourself up for a failure. A house is a product and it should be marketed as such. It helps when you have proper systems in place. Rick knows that – he and his team teach them to other estate agents (even former competitors). This strategy turns their competitors into collaborators. Clients benefit, because they have more agents working for them; estate agents win, because they have more properties to sell and better marketing strategies to use. Thanks to that, PPC and LM continually reinforce their position in the market.

"If you offer more, you can get more," summarises Rick. But you have to be clever about it. The key to success is to be confident enough to give your ideas away, but to charge for implementation. This makes you stand out, because you no longer compete on price (which is a very risky strategy, as you have to have volume to survive and it usually turns out quite hard to achieve). Rick's strategy makes you sell your brand rather than price. You sell value. You get yourself known, build up your assets and confidently operate in the market.

WHY A BRAND HERO?
The team, led by Rick, has a clear vision of how the industry can be improved and they do it in such a way that it benefits not only them, but clients and their former competitors (I say former, because they effectively become their business partners). By realising their vision, they are introducing a new quality to how the business in this niche is being done. They do not shy away from modern means of communication, but face-to-face contact with clients is still a very important part of this business. In addition, Rick is still involved in the day-to-day so he does not lose touch with reality.

MY LESSONS FROM THIS CONVERSATION
1. No strategy will tell you if you have a good product or not
2. Good strategy is necessary to get your product out there
3. Constant self-development is necessary to staying on top of trends but you need to choose techniques that fit to your business

INSPIRATION
Oversubscribed by Daniel Priestley

ELEMENTS OF A STRONG BRAND
- HAVING A PLAN
- BRAND IS IN STRATEGY AND PRODUCT
- GIVING VALUE AND MAKING SURE YOU RECEIVE VALUE AS WELL

MOTTO
"The quality of your life will be in direct proportion to the questions you ask" ~ *Tony Robbins*

FIND OUT MORE
- visit premiumpriceconsultants.co.uk
- visit londonmls.co.uk
- visit remarkablesgroup.co.uk
- Find Rick on LinkedIn /in/ricktooley/

What is your brand asking for?

DARSHANA UBL

Name: Darshana Ubl
Years in business: 12 years' property investing, 10 years' business leadership
Speciality: *"I'm in the business of helping small business"*
Location: London
Reach: International
Key to success: Triple win™ (win for the business, win for the client and win for the ecosystem – refer to Darshana's book *Triple Win* for details on this methodology)
Greatest asset: IP

WIN, WIN, WIN: THE DARSHANA EFFECT

For the record, Darshana Ubl is one person.

Lovely to talk to, a kind spirit, a loving wife, shrewd investor, keynote speaker and a proficient businesswoman with entrepreneurial personality. She has the personality of a she-wolf: nurturing and caring, but standing her ground if need be.

When I met her, I experienced her kindness and humour first. Then, as the conversation progressed, I knew I had better pay attention, for the fear of missing out. But that's just it – this worry was futile. She has an ability of making sure each conversation is a win-win situation. Or, actually, a win-win-win I should have written, but more about this later.

I've just realised that what I am about to write may feel as if I am developing a crush. And you know what? I am – on a professional level. To me, Darshana is so easy to look up to and so hard not to be written about in superlatives.

Commodity

Freedom, independence, individuality – no society can fully guarantee you will be able to enjoy them fully. Even when lawfully guaranteed, there are sociological and economical aspects to consider and – often – to overcome; then there is also a matter of choice. Darshana Ubl made up her mind early on – whatever choices she was to make in life, they would be her own.

In the culture she grew up in, that meant gaining financial independence. Even if your family was well situated, you had to make it on your own. Otherwise, women in India do not really have much room to manoeuvre and she was not prepared to settle just yet.

Do not limit yourself by being a talent

While Darshana was studying for her master's degree at university, she took up a job as a radio disc jockey for India's top radio channel *Radio Mirchi*. It is here where the producer commented on her performance: *"There is a business side to you, don't limit yourself by being a talent."* She didn't.

Next step was key account management at Singapore's number one TV channel, MediaCorp TV. It's here that Darshana truly developed her understanding of the commercial world and how much more powerful understanding the 'pull' methodology and creating value is when compared to forceful selling. Later she went on to be General Manager of an events company in Singapore, learning new ropes and expanding the business into seven parts of the world.

In 2011, Darshana moved to the UK and started her business and embarked on the road of entrepreneurship.

Since then, she has had many successful ventures and sits on advisory boards of companies. Darshana's latest venture, Verve Rally – a luxury lifestyle brand which specialises in travelling by luxury cars – not only focuses on bringing her clientele closer to fulfilment, but also gives back to nature, due to its carbon-neutral initiative.

Whatever she does she shines the light on, but she focuses on designing the experience rather than just being the talent.

Businesswoman helping entrepreneurs

I ask her whether she defines herself as a businesswoman more than an entrepreneur. Or, rather, a businesswoman with an entrepreneurial approach/philosophy. Someone who understands the importance of creating new possibilities, development and idea generation, as well as appreciating the challenges of being focused on one business and making it grow by focusing on the systems, funding, teams and leadership.

"When I first got into business I thought it was about being your own boss. But to be good in business you need to understand it's about helping others. Understanding your clientele. And you don't have one boss, you have many bosses. When you look at it that way you understand that business is to serve. And when you do a good job of that you notice that you get rewarded, and that is where your turnover comes in. The more you serve, the more you get rewarded."
~ Darshana Ubl

This philosophy makes business less transactional and more human – ultimately leading to an environment where the business wins, the client wins and society benefits as well. That is her own business methodology, which she describes in her book *Triple Win*™.

I understand it as an entrepreneurial interpretation of the three Ps of sustainability (people, planet, profit) combined with the best practices of negotiation: compromise is a failure – there is a way of finding the best solution for all involved. This methodology can be applied to start-ups and established corporations alike. If you ask me, the sooner, the better.

Darshana is going to continue helping post-revenue business develop even further, just in a new format. Working for businesses and creating businesses herself, she is well placed for this role. Even more than that, this is what she wants to do the most.

She notices the potential of people behind the business. She identifies which elements they need to grow, including cultural aspects of both the business and its audience, and directs them towards the components, allowing them to move to the next level. She combines a shrewd business mind, a tactful approach and incredible experience.

She could have stayed in her home country and had a comfortable life. She didn't. She still wanted security, but on her own terms. So, she went and got it.

"There's no 'right time', there's just 'right time for you'" ~ Darshana Ubl

WHY A BRAND HERO
I understand that this article may seem to be focused more on an individual journey than a brand, but in Darshana's case, this is a story of how a strong personal brand came into being. Whenever you meet her – it's just that. You meet HER. And with time the experience gets richer and richer.

There are some quotes and books you read which have the voice of their authors – whatever Darshana creates has that same effect. She develops her brand elegantly, with clarity, consistency and grace. She's kind and clever. It's worth paying attention to what she's up to, because it's almost as if she can make the time be right for her.

A personal brand worth learning from.

MY LESSONS FROM THIS CONVERSATION
1. Know your stuff, learn and grow and you will be able to create the right time for your next step [or] Remember the tough times, they will make your good times even more successful
2. Serve a purpose, it will make it easier for you to create value for yourself, your clients and the ecosystem
3. Be reasonable but do not let the doom and gloom of the economic climate sway you

ELEMENTS OF A STRONG BRAND
- INTEGRITY
- (COM)PASSION
- DETERMINATION

"A bird sitting on a tree is not afraid of the branch breaking, because its trust lies not on the branch but on its own wings"
~ one of Darshana Ubl's favourite quotes

INSPIRATION
- Tesla, their mission and the way they choose their partners
- Lego
- *The Alchemist* by Paulo Coelho

MOTTO
"Live. Love. Embrace life. Leave the planet a better place."

P.S. She says there aren't enough female role models out there. She admits that in her youth the choice was pretty much between an Iron Lady and a militant career woman. Today we have a few more choices, including celebrities, but a few she-wolves of business should be added into the mix. Now we know there is at least one.

Find out more
- Visit her official website darshanaubl.com
- Find her on LinkedIn linkedin.com/in/darshanaubl
- See what she's up to on Facebook facebook.com/DarshanaUbl
- Follow her on Twitter @DarshanaUbl
- Follow her on Google+
- ...and watch her TEDx talk *The Triple Win Effect*
- *Triple Win*™ book coming soon

What does your brand rely on?

MARCUS UBL, VERVE RALLY

Name: Marcus Ubl. At time of writing main brand he is involved in is Verve Rally, which he co-created with Darshana Ubl
Years in business: Verve Rally has existed since 2016; however, Marcus has been an entrepreneur since 2001
Speciality: Making brands fun to work in and work with
Location: London
Reach: Global
Key to success: Stay ahead, see the future and make it happen by shaping the day
Biggest challenge for businesses: The business he shares with his partner that already has a loyal following (I would also add, as it is mentioned more than once in the conversation: being able to assemble a team believing in the brand)

SEE THE BIG PICTURE, MANAGE THE DETAILS

With generations of business people in the family, it was almost an expectation that Marcus was going to follow that path. However, Marcus embraced it gladly, as for him, being in business – entrepreneurship, with its ups and downs – was a natural way to independence, flexibility and value creation. For himself, and also others.

"I got into business right after university at the age of 21 as I wanted to be in charge of my own destiny. My ambition is to provide value to the world by solving meaningful problems and get rewarded along the way."
~ Marcus Ubl

Discussion about the importance of nurturing culture in an organisation flows naturally – it is about integrity, values, communication with your team. That is what I call brand thinking.

It is also about realising that ultimately the market is going to verify your vision. It is always easier to support your business when you have the right tools and systems in place that in the core support your vision and philosophy. They all need to be aligned, otherwise there is no success. Observe, learn, adapt, repeat – always staying true to your values.

I first met Marcus when he was co-founder and director of Dent (then known as Entrevo) and what I learned about him then is as true today, when he develops Verve Rally (the first carbon-neutral rally in Europe). Brands he is involved in constantly learn and adapt – incremental innovation. And that is not just theory. What they preach they practise themselves.

"If you are going to learn from someone, see that they are getting the results you aspire to. If they are not, then moderate their advice."
~ Marcus Ubl

Verve Rally is an innovation in the European market for two reasons: they are the first carbon-neutral rally in Europe and they are also combining the best of two worlds – dynamism and luxury – uniting Marcus's passion for cars with his talent for connecting people in a nurturing environment.

They excite and deliver experiences, captivating imaginations, making those who haven't been on their rally yet want to go, and those who have been want to go again. They have already created a group of enthusiastic followers – a group that is rapidly growing.

What I am most impressed by is the scope of the experience they provide. I felt embraced by the brand even before I crossed the threshold of one of Verve's introductory evenings. The choice of location, style of communication, clips they share on social media, atmosphere during the evening, choice of business partners, follow-up information... it is all presented – and received – as part of a greater creation, giving you glimpses of what the actual trip may look and feel like. I, as a member of an audience, was very pleased for Verve to share their ideas and plans with me – and from the responses I heard around me, so were the other members of the audience.

Their logo is an emblem reminiscent of a luxury car badge – spot on. I encourage you to sign up to their newsletter; you will see how communication with the audience can be done elegantly and effectively. This brand had a very dynamic birth and is growing at an energetic pace. I attribute the tempo of this success not only to a fantastic and viable idea, but to experience of its co-creators. Especially when you can already consider Verve Rally as a brand with international presence. Grabbing too big a market too soon can often lead to a business being perilously stretched, and growing a brand too fast can lead to its dilution. Verve is developing fast, but not hastily, and this makes all the difference: the control is there and they are growing by design. Both co-creators have rich experience in growing global brands and this is visible through Verve's comprehensive experience and consistent progression.

"A brand creates an emotive sense of an intangible idea – noticeable at every touchpoint." ~ Marcus Ubl

Verve seems to be a brand of (e)motion. Marcus is a master of understanding which systems to put in place in order not to let the emotions run wild and overrun the brand. He makes it real enough so that the idea can be shared with others. He keeps it human. Clients remember that. It makes the experience memorable and even more valuable, and people notice that.

My advice – make sure there is someone like Marcus building your brand.

WHY A BRAND HERO?

Having a grand idea and still being able to connect with people on a 1-2-1 basis is an amazing skill. Marcus, as a personal brand, is an elemental ingredient for this formula to work. He is one of the people you find yourself looking up to, because they see what he can accomplish... not to mention the knowledge, skill and wit. He's an incredibly smart guy who makes you want to try harder to create something good. I certainly felt that as our conversation was energising and motivating.

And the best thing? When he sees that, he simply says *"cool"*.

He is definitely one person I constantly learn from. Instead of creating a business, Marcus co-created an adventure and that is what makes them my brand heroes.

MY LESSONS FROM THIS CONVERSATION

1. Every business needs a person like Marcus; they ground the mission, streamline development and allow the business to scale
2. Tools and systems support the heart of a business, they allow it to perform and grow
3. Systems aligned with brand values create an enhanced customer experience, make operations efficient and create value inside your business

ELEMENTS OF A STRONG BRAND

- INEEDS TO BE PERSONABLE
- CREATES A RELATIONSHIP WITH THE CLIENT
- FUTURE, VISION OF THINGS TO COME

INSPIRATION

- Elon Musk, who combines Nikola Tesla's brilliance with Jobs' or Edison's business savvy, is not afraid to look at things differently and relentlessly to makes things happen
- Lean start-up methodology
- Jeff Bezos

MOTTO

"See the big picture and manage the detail"

FIND OUT MORE
- Follow Marcus on Twitter @marcusubl
- Visit ververally.com
- Follow @Ververally
- Watch them on Instagram instagram.com/ververally
- Sign up to their newsletter ververally.com/#contact

Can you see a big picture?

ED VICKERS, JOLLIE'S

Name of business: Jollie's
Founder: Ed Vickers
Years in business: Since 2012
Speciality: *More-than-profit movement* to get homeless back on their feet using the medium of socks (to start with)
Location: London
Reach: National
Key to success: Partnerships
Greatest asset: Friendships

SOCK UP

The tube's on strike. Still, it is a lovely day. We meet at a café in Kensington, not too far from Jollie's HQ at The Refinery.

Ed Vickers created the brand while studying Bioscience at the University of Exeter. He wasn't that into it, but he got a 2:1 because he *"doesn't like not finishing things"*. During his studies, he volunteered at a homeless charity and an awareness began to grow of the need to make a change lasting longer than a few spare coins could provide. So he created Jollie's, an online shop selling socks.

I could say it is all about super funky socks, manufactured from ethically sourced materials, with eccentric names and packaged in quirky tubes. That would be intriguing, but I would only be telling a part of the story. The fact is, the socks are only the beginning.

Heart of gold

Every time you buy a pair of socks from Jollie Goods, you are giving a pair to a charity supporting the homeless in stepping out of the circle of poverty.

This is a key element of this idea. Ed's socks are not a cotton equivalent of a few spare coins you give away, because the sight of a homeless person at a corner of a street made you feel uncomfortable enough.

It is about education and knowing who you are helping, what your socks are helping people achieve.

Practical kindness

Jollie's cooperate with carefully selected charities that help the homeless write CVs, dress for an interview, and improve their skills. You can see the list on their website and soon you will be able to read the stories of people whose lives this deed has actually improved. It may have started as a random act of kindness, but with each pair sold it evolves into a purposeful action with a very tangible outcome: it becomes a reminder that the homeless are humans; and it reminds them of that as well.

Ed expressed a very important thought. There is no such thing as *the homeless*. It is not a homogenic category. There are soldiers, graduates, young adults... Yes, addiction is one of the most common causes of homelessness. But the circumstances vary. They can be changed – if we make an effort to recognise the human underneath the rags. That is what Jollie's are about.

Their ambition is to cooperate with businesses, educators and mentors to create more accessible training facilities, enabling people who lost their homes discover and develop skills to get a job, start a business, learn. Jollie's want to create an environment motivating that change and facilitating the development.

They start with socks.

WHY A BRAND HERO?

I believe all businesses should be social. It should not be the duty of corporate social responsibility policies to make businesses realise they can make a difference, that they are on a mission. It should be woven into the DNA of the brand, underlining its actions and relationships with clients and employees alike.

"A more-than-profit enterprise." I found this phrase on their website and I think it is an excellent way of describing how brands should think about themselves. There is nothing wrong with making money, but it can be achieved in so many ways – yet it is so much easier to make money if people don't mind you doing so and support you on the way, isn't it? It makes absolute sense: earning money is good as long as you're spending it in a good way.

MY LESSONS FROM THIS CONVERSATION
1. Doing good things is fun
2. You can do good, whatever your background
3. Do good now, don't waste time

ELEMENTS OF A STRONG BRAND
- **RELATIONSHIPS, GOOD PEOPLE WILL HELP YOU GET FURTHER**
- **UNDERSTANDING OF THE PEOPLE THE BRAND SERVES**
- **HUMILITY: ACHIEVING AND STILL WANTING TO ACCOMPLISH MORE**

At the time of the conversation Ed was a year out of uni... a year!

INSPIRATION
- the Stove Team (stoveteam.org)

MOTTO
"We make a living by what we get, but we make a life by what we give."
~ Winston Churchill

FIND OUT MORE
- Visit their website jolliesocks.com
- Facebook profile facebook.com/JollieGoods
- Follow them on Twitter @jolliegoods
- Instagram page instagram.com/jolliegoods

How much good does your brand do?

LUCY WILLIAMS, MY HEART SKIPPED PHOTOGRAPHY

Name of business: My Heart Skipped Photography
Founder: Lucy Williams
Years in business: Since 2005
Speciality: Portrait and wedding photography
Location: London
Reach: International
Key to success: Being ready to grasp the opportunity
Biggest challenge for businesses: Find your focus
Greatest asset: Unique outlook and character

THE POWER OF LOVE

My Heart Skipped HQ is in London, so we were able to meet face to face. This happened in one of the stylish Soho cafés. Even though we've never met before, there is no mistaking Lucy for someone else. She has a great smile and a cool look with artsy-vintage-funk about her.

We sit down, order a coffee and a smoothie and talk. After 15 minutes, it feels as if it's our weekly catch-up. We've only just met and yet it seems as if we know each other, and well. It is an open, candid conversation about the origins of My Heart Skipped Photography and about Lucy's coming into her own as a brand.

True colours

At the age of eight Lucy decided to become a painter. In the sixth form there was an option to do photography as GCSE alongside the A Levels English, French and Art. The school wouldn't let her. However, the teacher told her *"if I just happen to leave the paperwork out and you happen to find it and you happen to leave your application on my desk by the deadline, then I will enter you".* Even though officially she wasn't allowed to do this. The next day the paperwork was there, she got all the work in and spent a glorious September in the dark room. The discussion about the education is too big to even begin at this point, and probably deserves a book on its own…

Anyway, it was off to art college. Fate would have it that Lucy became allergic to paint. She returned to photography and what she would paint she took pictures of. Subjects closest to her heart: statements about the body and feminine art.

Snap, and you see it all

Photography led her to a job of scouting locations. Landscapes, spaces, places. That was another beginning. Love for the view through the lens grew.

Observing beautiful nature, creating, composing, telling stories. That was her way of becoming a photographer. Then it matured to become a business. Lucy is still perfecting her business model to accommodate new ventures.

It is a crowded marketplace, but she did find a differentiator. Actually, she discovered the differentiator that has been in her all along. For Lucy, to make a great portrait is to discover a spark within her subject. She lets them be. She is interested in discovering how people are.

Her favourite clients are the ones that say *"I hate having my picture taken". "For me, photography is about making a connection,"* says Lucy.

She takes herself and the camera out of the way. This enables her clients to see something in themselves that not many people have noticed and even fewer of them captured. She makes them beautiful by finding their true image. She calls it their sparkle.

"People just do not know what they have. I want to find out about their person, discover their little looks and what makes them smile. Then capture that." ~ Lucy Williams

So you meet Lucy, you chat. She is painting you through the lens. She studies you to discover the best features. Some do it via hair and make-up, she does it via observation. It's a collaborative process. At a portrait shoot she's not creating a person, but discovering the very glamorous them that is already there.

Lucy finds people in themselves, so to speak. She uses the lens as a medium to show their real faces. Pretence and studied poses leave her studio as she works with the client. And so with her brand, too. Clear, honest, with its own character. You can see it clearly on her website – easy to navigate and not imposing, but light – and it shows you all you need to know, at a glance.

Many beginnings

It seems that My Heart Skipped Photography have had many beginnings, but all ended up in love. Sometimes the relationship is, well, emotional, but it is always authentic.

WHY A BRAND HERO?

The fact that Lucy falls in love with her brand over and over again is fascinating. This romance leads her to discover new products and services. She does wedding photography all over the world, portraits and dating photography – again, her products are focused on illustrating the love in the world.

Her knowledge and passion are unquestionable, admirable and enviable. She finds that spark in the subjects of her photographs; actually, let me rephrase that – she has the spark herself, and through her products and delivery she devises a way of igniting it within her clients. She's the type of photographer that will help you look like you on a picture. That's no mean feat. Plus, she is adamant about evolving her brand and making it better; she's active in searching for ways which keep her brand relevant and true to its core values. And that is why she and her My Heart Skipped Photography are my brand heroes.

MY LESSONS FROM THIS CONVERSATION

1. There may be many beginnings to your brand, but it's the road towards the happy ending that counts

2. Passion trumps allergies (if you really care about something, you will find a way to make it happen)
3. Opportunities are out there, you'd better be ready when they come

ELEMENTS OF A STRONG BRAND
- **LOVE OF THE CRAFT**
- **LOVE OF THE CLIENT**
- **LOVE OF MAKING THE WORLD A BETTER PLACE**

MOTTO
"It's one thing to make a picture of what a person looks like, it's another thing to make a portrait of who they are" ~ Paul Caponigro

FIND OUT MORE
- Call +44 (0) 7968 097 219
- Email hello@myheartskipped.co.uk
- Tweet @myheartskipped
- Skype myheartskipped
- Follow facebook.com/myheartskipped
- Visit myheartskipped.co.uk

What do your clients see when they look at your brand?

RICH WITH, GROW CO.

Name of business: Grow Co.
Founder: Rich With & Mike Shelley
Years in business: Since 2005
Speciality: Grow Co. was founded in 2014, Rich has been making his mark on the industry for over 20 years
Location: Leigh-on-Sea
Reach: National
Key to success: Enjoy what you do
Biggest challenge for businesses: Not appreciating your brand
Greatest asset: Being willing

BE CREATIVE AND LAUGH

I met Rich at an event for young aspiring entrepreneurs where he presented his laws of design and branding. He was cool, confident, creative, reasonable and respectable, and he rocked the content. His delivery was smooth, filled with humour and practical anecdotes. This clearly was a guy who knew his stuff. I followed him... well, on social media. I signed up to his newsletter, as it was witty and knowledgeable. Then, when it came to this project, he was one of the first names on the list.

I meet him in his new studio in picturesque Leigh-on-Sea. It is a bright space, faithful to corporate colours of the brand, but this does not feel austere or restraining. It fits. It's a kind of space you want to be in. There are workspaces in the centre and people focused on their monitors. When they say *"Hi!"*, they smile.

There is a little kitchen where you can find more bicycles than plates, and a cosy garden where we begin our conversation. A quarter of an hour in we move inside as it starts to rain; however, the drops did not dampen the mood.

Rich brand design has always been the lead theme in Rich's rich career. He began designing newspapers and later on experienced several iterations of design business, both as a leader of a team and a solopreneur and freelancer. It can be a solitary experience, quite alienating.

"Working in a team, feeding ideas to each other, there's a community, a good group propels you forward. It gives you speed and reach and stronger foundations that you would not be able to achieve on your own. You learn new stuff, become better, faster, you progress. You grow. And so you can help you clients to grow, too." ~ Rich With

That seems to be, incidentally, the mission of Grow Co., as the name itself suggests. The trick is to grow keeping your soul in the process. Not installing processes for the sake of formalisation, but making sure that the system really works.

I can see that working with Grow Co. Their setting is not formal, yet everything has its space. From the meeting desk, to the workstations to the bikes. Well, almost. The team's bikes are parked in the kitchen area, but even that fits nicely within the atmosphere of the place. Nothing is in the way; what needs to be there, is.

Grow Co. are proficient in digital design, and what fascinates me about them is their love of print design that underlies it all. Print design is something you can hold in your hand – it makes your creativity tangible, makes your ideas something you can touch and feel and gives your project closure; it gives you an opportunity to really touch something you imagined, that speaks to you. I share that.

Grounded creativity, consistent performance. They have a neat spot in Leigh-on-Sea and this physical exposure helps. You can see their sign from the street and neat white and yellow space invites you in. Their branding, the atmosphere they create, is consistent inside and out; witty and neat. It gives you a taste of what sort of character you are going to meet and suggests a line of thinking as well.

"We like to be as creative as we can. But this is a project for them [clients]." ~ Rich With

They approach every project from the client's point of view.

And they speak many languages – from the elegant to grunge. I think this versatility became their house style. And dedication. And a certain level of funk. Each language has dialects, after all. It works – clients stay with them. There is a relationship and a growing one.

What I like about them is that they do not really get flustered by other *big* agencies. They do their thing. They are focused on doing it really, really well.

When a business comes to them it is a very exciting process. They want to create something great. It's emotional as well. And they are a part of the process. By keeping the personality in the loop they are creating something special. You can feel the buzz in the room; even if everyone is working quietly, you see they are engaged.

Consolidating the image

That includes the clients. They get immersed in the process and are opening up to the idea of a brand rather than a detached design of a solitary element. They welcome the opportunity to talk about their brand. It's a growing theme. In the past people were developing compilations of elements with their logo on them; nowadays, they are more inclined to develop a brand. And they welcome the conversation. It's a good trend and it's great that Grow Co.'s clients are a growing part of it.

Being different is finally being perceived as a good thing and businesses are honing in on that. They are brands and they want to express themselves as such.

Don't fake it, make it

Being a brand allows you to grow. Trying to become one at all costs doesn't.

"We want them to be involved. Take responsibility for what they are doing. Talking about branding means, to some extent, giving business advice. We see what works what doesn't. As far as brand is concerned."
~ Rich With

Next step is to just grow.

Keep it lifestyle
Keep evolving
Keep growing
Inspire
Work with characters

Small businesses can look like their biggest competitors. Grow Co. root for the underdog. They make the most of it and they enjoy what they do.

WHY A BRAND HERO?

From Post-it caricatures to rebranding organisations, they do it with knowledge and passion.

They are quietly confident. You know they know about their craft. The portfolio speaks for itself. They are confident enough to tell you what they really think. The honest delivery is what seems to be at the core of the brand. For the ability of creating awesomeness that speaks volumes, even if it's subtle, they are my brand hero.

Also, talking to them made me smile.

MY LESSONS FROM THIS CONVERSATION
1. You have a potential to be a brand, harness it
2. Have fun
3. Introduce systems when it's appropriate

ELEMENTS OF A STRONG BRAND
- PERSONALITY
- FUN
- EXCITEMENT
- ORIGINAL
- CLEVER
- NICHE

INSPIRATION
- *Made in Leigh* newspaper
- *The 22 Immutable Laws of Branding* by Al Ries and Laura Ries

Made in Leigh is an eye candy, and full of substance, too.

MOTTO
"Be creative and laugh."

FIND OUT MORE
- Visit their website justgrow.co
- Find them on Facebook facebook.com/JustGrowCo
- Follow them on Twitter @JustGrowCo
- Discover them on LinkedIn linkedin.com/company/5050198
- Watch them on Instagram instagram.com/justgrowco/
- Pin them on Pinterest pinterest.com/justgrowco

How would you like to grow your brand?

LEVENT YILDIZGÖREN, TTC WETRANSLATE

Name of business: TTC wetranslate
Founders: Banu Yildizgören and Levent Yildizgören
Years in business: Since 1995
Speciality: Technical, legal and marketing translations
Location: Chelmsford
Reach: International
Key to success: Doing the best you can
Biggest challenge for businesses: Managing red tape while staying competitive and innovative
Greatest asset: Enthusiasm for the industry

CONTEXT MIGHTIER THAN WORDS

In 2012 I used to work at a company based three buildings down from what was then TTC's headquarters. I even once used their services to translate my university documents. I remember their service to be prompt and efficient. I have also heard good words about them from my colleagues and then I started noticing Levent's posts on a business portal of which we are both members. Our paths crossed only recently when TTC took over a smaller translation agency and approached me to help them with their brand unification strategy. This gave me an opportunity to get to know them and they have made an impression big enough for me to want to share it with you.

DON'T GET LOST IN TRANSLATION

They are a translations agency that use their expertise to boost the position of their clients' brands in global markets. I have never met a translator that had such a comprehensive and caring approach. What makes them stand out is that they care about their clients' businesses more than they care about the document they are translating (and they care about those a great deal). This means they look at the context of their translation, not just a simple transformation from one language to another. They work to make their clients' message clear in every language so that it is fit for purpose for the target countries. To me their brand stands for cultural context, professional expertise, industry knowledge.

First words

The brand grew from a living room business led by Banu, the co-founder. It grew organically and when they won a big order, her husband, Levent decided it was time for him to join in, so he left his job in print and to this day he has been Managing Director of the business. Still, the values that made them care about translations then are present in the business now.

They are experts in technical translations across sectors and understand how challenging it can be for a brand to get their message across clearly. Indeed, they are in a process of polishing their own communication style as well. This makes them a unique partner to their clients, and it is impressive that they have always thought about themselves as partners for their clients – cooperation, relationship building and sharing their expertise freely are embedded in TTC's culture.

TLC[1] of TTC

Levent says the two things of which he is most proud about his brand is that they are still growing as a business and that they were able to build a team that truly cares. He has seen evidence of them going beyond what duty requires to keep their clients happy. I have seen evidence of that myself. Even though they are working with a network of hundreds of linguists, there is a camaraderie, a family atmosphere within the team. They want to make a difference, whether it is a job or a community support challenge that requires them to (or gives them an opportunity to) dress up as Minions, they want to really make an impact and change things for the better.

They want to continue growing, making a bigger impact, and keep making themselves known, one job well done at a time.

....
1   An acronym of Tender, Loving Care

WHY A BRAND HERO

They are a close-knit team who give their best. Levent's dedication for the business is inspiring and he definitely leads by example. They make time to share knowledge in order to streamline their clients' processes. Admirable.

The fact that they refuse to just go the easiest way and instead choose to do the right thing, find out about the context of the translation and get to know their clients' brands – combined with their industry experience – makes them a unique and valuable partner to any business. That is why they are my brand hero. For their modesty, comprehensive approach and appreciation of a brand.

MY LESSONS FROM THIS CONVERSATION

1. Love what you do, it will not help you avoid the difficult times, but it will help you go through them; without the passion, it's not worth doing
2. Build a team that cares, you will motivate each other and rise to the top together
3. Work with your clients, become partners, it's much more valuable to them

ELEMENTS OF A STRONG BRAND

- **ENGAGEMENT**
- **CARE FOR THE CLIENT, CARE FOR THE JOB**
- **COMMUNITY PRESENCE, AWARENESS OF THEIR ROLE AND DOING THEIR BIT**

INSPIRATION

- Richard Branson for the way he develops his brands
- Daniel Priestley for showing small and medium businesses, even start-ups and solopreneurs, how to think big

MOTTO

"Make successes personal and approach problems professionally."

FIND OUT MORE

- Visit their website ttcwetranslate.com
- Follow them on Twitter @lovetranslation
- Find them on Facebook @TTC.Language.service

*What is the
language of your
brand?*

CONCLUSION

BRAND HEROES: THE IDEAL AND THE PRACTICAL

There you have it. Stories of real-life brands that I see as heroes. I see their powers. I defined them in the introduction and, so far, I characterised 10:

1. Brand heroes inspire culture
2. Brand heroes stand proudly next to their logo
3. Brand heroes know how to learn from mistakes
4. Brand heroes are open to knowledge
5. Brand heroes are sanely passionate about what they do
6. Brand heroes are purposeful
7. Brand heroes have a firm grasp of reality
8. Brand heroes have appetite for solutions they can deliver today
9. Brand heroes champion cooperation
10. Brand heroes grow

Although the 10 together create an avatar of a brand hero, I find that usually one or two characteristics dominate in real-life brand heroes: such as Aaron, who inspires culture, or Marcus Ubl, for whom systemised knowledge is a key characteristic. That may be due to the features of their chosen industry or due to the maturity of their brand in the market. Thus, I chose champions who, to me, seem to be sporting each trait most prominently, and explained how I see them within the context of their brand.

1. Brand heroes inspire culture

Creating a culture within an organisation seems to be the ultimate corporate goal, and there are systems and strategies that can assist in summarising it and introducing it to new members of an organisation. Still, it seems that brand heroes are doing it instinctively. They themselves, as individuals, are ambassadors of their brands. They symbolise the very idea behind the business. They live and breathe the business, creating the environment others want to join. They do not have to take the market by storm – the market joins them, because they represent something worthwhile, that resonates with a very specific group of people. Their audience shares their values. I believe brand heroes become beacons to their audiences' beliefs.

That is how employees who believe in those brands are able to find them as well. I see a difference between hiring people and engaging them. With the former, you get people to do a job, micromanage them between 9 and 5, while they wait to get back to doing what they really like after hours, and you notice that they cannot wait for the end-of-shift bell to ring. With the latter, you find people that resonate with you on the level of values and buy into your vision. Prime examples of this practice are Aaron and the Fikay concept, TTC wetranslate and Zandra Rhodes' studio. They apply it out of their own will: they find tasks to bring the team closer to achieving that great goal of bettering the brand, and themselves in the process. Creating a culture means creating a symbiotic relationship between team members and the brand. It is about appreciating individual talents and creating space for them to grow – allowing them to develop themselves for the benefit of the whole organisation.

2. Brand heroes stand proudly next to their logo

Consider your logo an element of heraldry: it is an emblem giving viewers a glimpse of your values, beliefs, history, current position and ambitions. The colours, the typeface, the balance of shapes, whether the corners are soft and rounded or sharp, how you display your credo... It is a symbol of what you, your brand, represent. Although a logo and a brand name are not enough to 'be a brand' or 'have a brand', these are two important elements of it. They matter, because what they represent is so very precious. Therefore, every element (shape or word) you choose to include in it should have a purpose and be there for a reason. There is no place for superfluity in a logo, as it serves a precisely defined purpose: it is a doorway into a brand.

During my interviews I found that for brand heroes a logo is a badge of honour. When you look at the brand you can see the founder, and by interacting with the founder you can see elements of the brand: that is what the alignment of values and vision means. Each strengthens the other. Emma Stroud with Pitch Perfect Club, Emma Davidson with Affinity Capital, and Holly Helt with Chiki Tea are great examples of that: their brands' approach to their client is very similar to how they approach people personally and you can gauge the tone of voice of the brand from the very first conversation you have with them. All elements are consistent, aligned and create a fantastic introduction into their culture and code of conduct.

3. Brand heroes make mistakes

As uncomfortable it may be, we all make mistakes because we try new things. Brand heroes stand out in the way they approach the consequences. Being imperfect does not stop them from trying to get better. I respect them immensely for that. It is not about fear of failure anymore. They try anyway. What is more, they seem to remove the term 'failure' not only from their vocabulary but from their thinking. It is not about being irresponsible or haphazard, but about taking calculated risks and going for it, listening to your instincts, then measuring the outcomes and improving upon them. To me, this is one of the bravest things to do.

Here's an example. Aseptium specialises in research and development of technologies for decontamination of complex surgical instruments. R&D is at the core of their activities and this very discipline is all about trying new things, prototyping new concepts, making mistakes, and being able to eliminate what does not work, adapt, change and try again. Making mistakes is never intentional but it happens because all assumptions need to be adjusted when approaching new projects. It is always a trade-off between the cost of prior research and the final outcome. But even Mark Zuckerberg says that *done* is better than perfect[1].

4. Brand heroes are open to new knowledge

There is a tool that counts how many blogs are being published on the web every day. It is now 12:14 am, 15th October 2016 and the counter has already reached 2,330,778. These are blogs, mixing professional and anecdotal content. Sifting thoroughly through it all

....
1   I haven't found that first speech/Facebook post with this quote - Google points towards various sources attributing this thought to Mark Zuckerberg. (If you happen to know the correct source, do let me know). He might not have been the first one to arrive at this conclusion, though. Either way, I agree with the sentiment.

is a challenge and I am not referring to this overwhelming number to simply show how accessible yet confusing reaching for information can be. Information becomes irrevocably cluttered, yet finding it is necessary. Brand heroes do it in a specific, selective way. They know what matters to them and their brands and they are very protective of their own time, so they spend it wisely on getting to information that is constructive and helps them serve their clients better. That also impacts how they present their information: no wasting time on faff. This applies to how they review the information as well, so bear this in mind when you are preparing to present to a brand hero.

Claudia Fallah (Claudia Fallah Cosmeceuticals), Pawel de Sternberg Stojalowski (Aseptium), Marcus Ubl (Verve Rally), and Heather Katsonga are further examples of brands for whom learning is a habit and who became an intrinsic part of their brand and growth strategy. It helps improve their products and services and enables them to discover new markets. For example, Aseptium recently found out about a mathematical model of infection spread used by veterinary scientists that could potentially be adapted and adopted to help hospitals improve their infection control systems, and Aseptium is to develop bespoke technologies based on this new data. Verve Rally, created by Marcus and Darshana Ubl, is a prime example of combining traditionally masculine motorsport with traditionally feminine luxury travel. Innovation is a fundamental part of their success. When it comes to Heather Katsonga, her thirst for knowledge is insatiable. When you look her up on Facebook or dive into the history of her blog entries, she is almost constantly studying, investigating, receiving certificates... That is part of her modus operandi: she chooses subjects that will elevate her brand to new heights and, in turn, her passion for making this happen becomes that much stronger.

5. Brand heroes are sanely passionate about what they do

Being good at what you do, even excellent at what you do, is not enough to succeed. Actually, it is not enough to even stick at it. If you do not love what you do, you will find an excuse to stop it. Perhaps it will not be at the first hurdle, because you will want to prove that you have tried, but soon enough. If you love what you do, you will use those hurdles to make the brand stronger. This passion is not blind, though. It is about understanding the context of the market, knowing the shortcomings of the brand and still caring for it, seeing its potential and giving it every chance to succeed, including your own hard work, sweat and tears (sometimes of joy). Entrepreneurial life is a rollercoaster and it can be a violent one. This feeling you get when you are on top of the world will help you remember to turn on the light when you find yourself at the bottom bend of the ride.

Sam Morris, Heather Barrie and Jane Malyon have each created a gem of a brand with a unique character and clearly stand out in the market. Sam with her adoration of fauna, Heather's uncompromising yet inviting approach to all things coffee and Jane's huggable Britishness of your favourite auntie. They are very aware of what the market may have in store. They are taking it by storm with their relentless hard work supported by their passion. It's a marriage of strong minds and strong hearts; one without the other could destabilise the performance of the brand, yet together they stabilise it, making it scalable and successful.

6. Brand heroes are purposeful

Having a vision is your *due north*, an ideal scenario, an image of your version of the future, of what you wish the world to be like. That is the ultimate inspiration that permeates through every element, system and person involved in it.

Mission helps to achieve the vision. It describes the current situation and the activities you undertake in order to change the world. Both together propel your brand forward. Having a vision does not mean you have everything figured out. It means that you have a direction. Actually, you are likely to meander off track every now and again, but a strong sense of knowing where you are going will help in figuring out how to overcome obstacles and get there in the end.

Haseena Latheef with DFY Norm, wearing her heart on her sleeve, has a powerful mission of promoting role models in our lives and adding authenticity to the sense and image of beauty. Her beliefs are very potent and the influence she has on her audience is mesmerising. Bigger start-ups could waver under the pressure of the fashion world. In addition to challenges, enterprises introducing new products to the market have to overcome logistics, supply, sometimes less than reliable service providers... Having a vision of where you wish to be gives you that power to burn the midnight oil, because at all times you know what and whom you are doing this for. As Simon Sinek would say: you understand your *why*.

7. Brand heroes have a firm grasp of reality

Brand heroes are on a quest to change the world and they recognise that the first step is to truly understand the state of affairs right here, right now. Only then can you really plot the course towards the coveted destination and make that all important first step, and make it steady.

Heather Barrie is one of the most down-to-earth people I know. With her, what you see is what you get, from hat to toe. Her insight into the inner workings of the coffee and hospitality industry is amazing. She does not sugar coat it but names it as it is. She also understands the potential for change. It will not happen overnight, but she relentlessly works towards overthrowing shit coffee providers, one cup at a time. Sonia Gill recognises the potential of her clients, as well. Working in the education sector with heads of schools, she shows them the path to achieving outstanding results. However, the start of that journey begins in the place they are at, and this means appreciation of what works and recognition of what needs improvement and, perhaps, pruning. Honest assessment provides clarity and creates space for changes to happen.

8. Brand heroes have appetite for solutions they can deliver today

None of us is ideal. Flawlessness can be paralysing. It's not what brand heroes are about. They are about being as good as you can be today, rather than being flawless tomorrow. It's about not letting what you haven't yet become block you from using what you have already achieved. Emma Stroud from Pitch Perfect Club knows that perhaps better than anyone else. She and her business partner liberate people's stories by freeing them from their fear of public speaking. Their clients start at various stages, depending on their skills and confidence, and they take it from there. Steven Briginshaw, through his experience, realised that having great potential can stop people in their tracks – too many things to do can be overwhelming!

Focusing on small things you can manage right now is much more effective than freaking out about great tasks you never get round to doing. From my own experience, writing a book is a daunting task. Writing a weekly blog, on the other hand, does not seem as scary in comparison, and is a good place to start. Otherwise, I would still be trembling under the looming task of having to start to write a book (and that would still, probably, be scheduled for tomorrow). Now, let's move on to the next thing.

9. Brand heroes champion cooperation

The 'self-made man' is a myth. As individuals we are influenced by other individuals around us; we constantly act and react as we are immersed in a society. We can only get so far if we try to go it alone. Being in business is hard enough, being adamant on being in it for yourself and doing everything alone means stretching yourself too thin and setting yourself up to fail. I do not know too many chocolatiers who are brilliant accountants and welders... do you? There are only so many hours in the day.

I also believe that trying to do everything yourself is ultimately selfish. We are all good at many things, but we are really excellent at a few at best. Making time to devote ourselves to pursuing that excellence seems logical, yet so often we sacrifice it to become mediocre in an activity we do not enjoy. It is not a way of serving our clients, creating a brand, or even leading a happy life.

Delegation is one thing. Cooperation is another. Sister Snog is the epitome of cooperation. Discovering people with talent and attitude to share it is what the brand is all about. The more confident you are about your own brand, the more attractive you are to potential strategic partners. It is easy for them to grasp the essence of your business and see how both sides could work together to amplify their position in the market: through referrals, business and brand support, improving the matrix of services...

There is also a way of looking at competition – if we switch to thinking about competitors as potential partners, and consider that working with them can benefit both us and them and elevate both brands to 11, we make the world a much better place. And, it can begin now.

10. Brand heroes grow

Have you ever seen this meme: *"growing old is inevitable, growing up is optional"*? It is a fitting summary of brand heroes' approach to time. They choose to progress, embracing the lessons along the way. Gosia Skibińska's story is a testament to this: her persistence in evolving her craft is admirable. Natalie Haverstock also impressed me with the story of her brand development, making the most of her skills as an actress and entertainer, determined to give the world a reason to smile.

Emma Louise Davidson, whom I see as an all-round role model, has proven to me how far you can go if you decide to utilise support you have around you. When I first met her, she was one of the 50-ish companies beginning a business accelerator course. Since then she has published a book and spoken in an auditorium filled with a few thousand guests, consistently delivering value through her brand.

ON THE WAY TO GREATNESS

We usually notice great brands around us when they are commercially successful and often have international reach. We rarely hear about their *road to greatness* and the issues they had to deal with and concepts they had to iron out. That does not mean, though, that they never had them. Therefore, no business should believe they are not good enough, because they still have processes to figure out, products to improve, early-day 'ups and downs' or are simply not big enough. It only means they are on the way there – and I believe they, with a bit of conscious effort, can certainly get there.

So, there you have it. I believe brand heroes can be found on all stages of entrepreneurial journeys. I see them all the time and it always amazes me that some of them are surprised by my assessment that they are brands already, saying I'm not doing anything special, I'm just doing what I love, and my clients seem to love it, too. And that is exactly what I find is special about them. These days good quality is ubiquitous (or rather communication focused on quality), so projecting just that is no longer enough. Brand heroes' passion gives them that extra credit needed to make them truly distinctive. They are being noticed by people who want to become their clients. Passion is that extra element that makes brand heroes even more successful. Their existence proves you can change the world for the better by doing what you love, because you are changing – improving – your own immediate environment. I am not saying that everything comes easy for them, far from it. As with any business, this labour of love requires a lot of work – hard work. Actually, it may be that it is a little easier for them to overcome challenges, after all. Bad days happen to all of us, yet brand heroes see them as part of the process, not the end. They are able to see that, because they believe in the cause, they believe in themselves, and when they feel weaker, they find someone or something to give them strength. They are able to do that because their passion attracts help from others that share their beliefs. It also catches the attention of clients who buy into their vision. They manifest their support by purchasing their products and services – and that carries them over to another day.

They have an understanding of their clients that leads to having an understanding with their clients. It is a partnership based on a union of goals, respectful analysis of problems, and an elegant environment of solutions that grow with the client. Brand heroes make sure everyone who meets them receives a bundle of value. Always.

Some of us are brand heroes already. Some of us are brand heroes in the making. I find it is easier to see a brand hero in someone else than in myself. Perhaps it is because with others I have the benefit of perspective. Perhaps in myself it is just easier to see how much can be done and what is not yet perfect. This at times gets overwhelming. Sadly, this also tints the bigger picture, taking the focus away from what already has been achieved and that should be celebrated a little, to give us a boost to push through the lows until the next high.

The trick is to teach yourself how to regain that perspective. Giving yourself permission to celebrate yourself can be tricky and is much harder than putting yourself in a negative light. Being constructively honest with myself, without putting myself down, is something I am constantly working on. Interviewing brand heroes was an excellent lesson for me.

That is why I decided to share this introspection method with you.

INTROSPECTION

A brand hero, inside out

To make it easier to highlight your achievements and to point out areas that can be improved, in order to grow into a brand hero, here are the questions I used during the interviews that created the basis for articles included in this book.

Use them to interview yourself.

There are no wrong answers.

Be honest to create an accurate picture. If you are on the beginning of your entrepreneurial journey, these answers may help you create a benchmark from which to grow your brand hero status. Whichever stage you are at right now, it is the best place to make the next step from.

To make this process easier I prepared a template of this self-interview that you can download from
www.incelement.co.uk/brand-heroes-the-book
this way you can be as creative as you want, not being limited by the size of the pages in this book.

WARM-UP QUESTIONS

List the facts and set the scene. If you are interviewing yourself in writing, it is a simple hack to just put something on a page. If you are talking to a voice recorder or being interviewed by a team member, these simple questions will help you... well, start talking. No editing at this point. No frowning at the sound of your own voice. Well, there may be a little frowning, but get over it and start talking (your voice may sound strange to you, but you have been talking to people for years and most of them have been talking back).

1. Your name
2. Name of the business
3. Years of operation
4. Location

5. Reach
6. Recent successes and/or accolades

NAMING

We know your name and it is now time to look closer and review its etymology. Remind yourself of the circumstances in which it happened – the place, time of day, who was there with you when you first thought of / heard / imagined / realised / wrote down the name…

7. How did you choose the name? Was there a process? If yes, what was it? Were there other people involved?
8. Why this one? What were your early intentions for the name to convey?

VISUAL IDENTITY

Think about the times before you had all the colours, typefaces and shapes figured out. Then consider how all the elements came into being and the people involved. How did you feel during that time: do you remember the excitement, perhaps impatience…? Try to remember the atmosphere during the process and dive into the questions below.

9. Describe your brand symbols and colours. Are they the same as when you started the business? If they evolved, what triggered it? When was it? Who was involved?

MISSION & VISION

Now it's time for the big guns. This section highlights the relationships between the founder and the business, so before you dive into analysing the business brand, consider your own values, beliefs and motivations – things you like best in life, things – and people – that truly matter in your life. Think about your family. Think about your favourite place in the world, your own corner in the world where you feel you truly belong. Think about your favourite movie and that scene that always makes you smile. When you're smiling, you are ready to get on with this section.

10. Why did you get involved in business in the first place?
11. What was it you want to change (in your industry)?
12. Why are you the one to make it happen?

13. How do you see your brand evolving in the future?
14. How do you see the industry growing/changing?
15. Is your business in line with your education/training?

VALUES

Keep thinking about your personal 'top 10 most excellent elements in the life of (insert your name here)' you created before the section above. Use that momentum to go through this part. Create a list of bullet points if it helps and then elaborate on them to see how matters important to you live in/through/despite/alongside your brand and then think about if/how they influence your business.

16. What personal values have you brought to your business that allowed it to grow?
17. Do you think it's necessary to have business and personal values aligned? Why?
18. What, in your opinion, constitutes a strong brand?

QUICK-FIRE

Relax, the hard part is over. This last part is the lightest of them all, although not completely without a challenge. I mean to say now it's time to allow yourself to turn down all filters. Write down or say whatever comes to mind first. Do not overthink this – just speak. Analyse the answers after the last question. The more candid you are, the more truthful – and even surprising – the answers will be. If it helps, give yourself 15 seconds to answer each question. Don't even think about getting ready. Just go ahead.

19. What is your greatest business ambition?
20. What is your greatest business fear?
21. Which business figure do you most identify with? Do you have brand heroes of your own (either commercial or personal brands)? What do you value them for? Why?
22. What trait is the hardest to overcome when running a business?
23. What is the trait that was the easiest to embrace when starting your business adventure?
24. What is the trait you most deplore in other businesses?
25. What's your brand's greatest success? How do you define success?
26. If you could change one thing about your business, what

would it be?
27. What is your most treasured business asset?
28. What do you regard as the lowest depth of misery?
29. What's business bliss?
30. What is your motto?

That's it.

I used this questionnaire to interview my brand heroes and it is equally useful as a template to interview your own brand: either write down the answers yourself or use it as a template for discussion during one of your core team briefings. Brand development is a function in time: businesses grow and their audiences mature; therefore, branding is never fully complete. What matters is that we can make brands as relevant and great as we can TODAY. With mission and vision in place we will be able to put ourselves in a place from which we can grow into an even better brand tomorrow.

When I work with my clients I always try to find out all that I can about them – as business brands and personal brands. It is like creating a map: the more I know, the wider the view (and I can also zoom in to see all the detail of the topography); understanding a brand's origin helps me understand how the clients are equipped to traverse the terrain; their vision tells me where they want to go, their mission – what stage of the journey they're at and values – what's the type of the adventure. As with any trip, it is good to get your bearings every once in a while, to check progress and make sure you are going in the desired direction.

Brand hero mirror

Now that you have pondered over the questions, I want to ask you which brand hero traits you find within yourself.

To sum up, you are a brand – as you are today, what will you make it look like tomorrow?

I believe, by learning from examples in this book, you can become an even better brand tomorrow. And what about being a brand hero? You are already on the way.

Thank you for reading. I truly appreciate you investing your time and journeying through these pages. May my musings give you a nudge to polish your brand. In the meantime, if you have comments, questions or would like to begin a brand conversation – get in touch:

Web: kdss.me
Facebook: www.facebook.com/KlementynadeSternbergStojalowska
LinkedIn: www.linkedin.com/in/klemens

Web: incelement.co.uk
Twitter @IncElement
Facebook: www.facebook.com/IncElement

Until then,

Kdj

Klementyna de Sternberg Stojalowska

ACKNOWLEDGEMENTS

Thank you, my Brand Heroes – past and present – you shared your stories with me, I learned so much.

Thank you, my teachers and mentors Daniel Priestley, Andrew Priestley, Darshana and Marcus Ubl and the Dent community.

Thank you to my husband, Pawel, for first edits and helping me keep this project constructive.

Thank you to Michele Ragozzino, Jeremy Siggers and Prof Jay Mitra for your comments and encouragement.

And, last but not least, thank you to those who gave me the first taste of this industry and made me fall in love with advertising and branding: Rafał Witkowski, Norbert Wawro, Aneta Rząca, Jarek Nakielny, Hanka Kukieła, Tomasz Horbaczewski, Michael Heidtman, Marcin Bieniek, Igor Banaszewski.

For all of you – and to all of you – I am grateful.

ABOUT THE AUTHOR

There are two great days in a person's life - the day we are born and the day we discover why. ~ William Barclay

1983 was a good year for me. A year when it all began – when I began – as I was born on 8th October in Kraków, Poland. I was born a second time, as a professional, in 2004. Then I started work as a copywriter in a full-service advertising agency.

[on the margin: Full service, in the context of an advertising agency, means they take care of the whole campaign process: from initial ideas, through strategy, production, implementation and, when required, follow up. This also means that they can engage with various media platforms, depending on client's requirements.]

Here I got immersed in the advertising alchemy, working on accounts for small, medium and huge brands with international presence, for instance BP, Tesco, Roca Poland, Novartis, Janssen Cilag, Grants. As one-half of a creative team I even won two industry accolades. Understanding big brand thinking (how they identify and express themselves, how they communicate and why they behave the way they do) was an important element of my professional development.

As for my education, I obtained a Masters Degree in Sociology from Jagiellonian University in Kraków. Sociology is a versatile, fascinating subject. You explore behaviours of groups and people, study their beginnings and developments, look at why and how relationships turn to networks and how institutions emerge. As such it lends itself nicely to branding. Both in case of a brand itself and it's clients. I have always been intrigued by why brands manifest themselves the way they do, what is the origin of their values and why they attract certain groups above others. This background helped me get a comprehensive, to unearth true values of a brand and motivations of an ideal client.

In the meantime I got married, moved to the UK and founded Inc Element providing creative branding solutions. You can say I was born for a third time… Initially this meant writing copy for

London-based agencies, creative adaptations and translations for brands including TK Maxx, BP. I continued to observe Britain's entrepreneurial scene and wanted to work directly with businesses. I also engaged with various networking groups and invested in business education – I am a proud alumni of Dent's Key Person of Influence.

alumnus

It was around that time that I had an idea to interview entrepreneurs and business owners with a view to investigate what makes a strong brand, be it a personal or a business one. Why have they gone into business in the first place, what do they believe in, what and whose problems are they solving, and how, and why... This project resulted in an unprecedented introspection, a behind-the-scenes-view of brands at different stages of maturity. We get to see them as they are now and also take a look at the process of their becoming. This observation led me to identify an archetype of, what I call, a Brand Hero. That in turn transformed into this book.

This research and experience led me to having been a Guest Lecturer at the University of Essex, helping MBA students with brand strategy and storytelling, speaking at Google Campus on the role of brand as a business asset (as part of a Migrant Business Accelerator), being a mentor to several start-ups (including med tech, personal development and creative sectors), leading a business networking group for Polish professionals in London and speaking on subjects of brand development, brand storytelling as well as brand communication and copywriting. It also inspired me to formulate a 5-step brand development methodology, so watch this SPACE!

For now, I live in the Scottish Highlands, with husband and two cats, where I enjoy the scenery, literary landscape, an occasional board game and a sci-fi box set.